# SHARING

## our stories, our selves, our success

### Volume 3

*an anthology*
*of women's empowerment stories*

# SHARING: *our stories, our selves, our success*
## Volume 3
### *an anthology of women's empowerment stories*

Canadian Cataloguing in Publication Data

SHARING: *our stories, our selves, our success*
ISBN 978-0-9940796-7-1


Editing, Layout and Design by
*words ... along the path*
a branch of One Thousand Trees


Printed in Guelph, Ontario, Canada by
M & T Printing Group

# Contents

# Wise Ones Dancing

I see who we are, oh magical ones
Traversing rocky paths,
Crossing countless lifetimes,
Glowing with such strength and depth and wisdom,
And yet bearing still the memory of a deep sadness
Which sometimes masks the freshness and joy
We brought with us here.

Perhaps we've forgotten
Or become tangled in the threads,
Lost site of the flow and rhythm
In a maze of cob web chains
Of choices, dreams and desires.
How do we hold onto the knowing
That all is the dance
And in its right place and time?

Last night, the full moon
Shone in through my bedroom window,
Nudging me, prodding me
To hold onto my intuition,
And to trust that I am always surrounded
By the strength and wisdom
Of those who love me,
Who have forever loved me,
Through all space and time.

... cont'd

La Luna,
A gentle reminder
That the lessons of others
Are also my teachings,
About standing my ground
While bending with the breeze,
Being both strong and vulnerable
To the pain, the joy and the glee
Of the dance.

The moon, urging me again to see
That parents, children, family, lovers and friends
Are my greatest teachers
For other wise, why would we be here
Dancing?

Reminding me
To always teeter on, even in the face of falls.
To cry, then laugh again,
Especially when the lights go out.
To spin and bend
And chase the scuttling clouds
Across a moody sky.
To scoop and gather them in my arms
When on a gem dazzled night,
They brush a brilliant, moon lit beach
With their shadowy breadth.

To look to the horizon for a brighter tomorrow,
Even while tightening my cloak
Against the sharp sting
Of a too cold wind.

... cont'd

And to remember that we are here,
Not only as models for one another,
But to dance on the head of a pin,
Reach for the top of the mountain,
Rest on a gentle slope,
Love and be loved
With a boundless passion and joy,
Delight in it all,

And to always recall
That as we are, we always shall be,
My friends, daughters, sons, mothers,
Oh, lovely admired ones,
Wise ones dancing.

**Love and blessings on the Journey**

**Barbara Lynn Andrew**
**March 2004 with many revisions.**

# Introduction

Three years ago, when I first got the idea to publish an anthology of women's empowerment stories, I would never have imagined the impact this project would have ... on me, on my writers, and on the people who purchased and read the book.

As an example, here is a comment from someone who read the first volume:

*The title of this book could not have been more appropriate. I found it truly amazing that so many women have shared their heart and soul in the well-written stories they have chosen to share with others. Writing these stories must have been both difficult and cathartic at the same time. Congratulations to each and every writer in this book, who was able to put pen to paper to share their story in such a way readers of your book can relate to. My blessings to you all; your stories are powerful and thought-provoking. I would recommend this book to anyone who is having difficulty in their life journey. I believe part of healing is being able to understand others have had similar experiences.*

And from a writer whose story was included in Volume 1:

*This journey of digging deep and sinking in has been utterly transformative ~ allowing old wounds to see the light of day and finally heal. I hope the words of these women resonate deeply and support others on their journey.*

I had never intended on publishing a men's volume .... that is, until a male friend of mine, who had read the women's book, suggested that I do so. "Are you going to write for me?" I asked him. When he unhesitatingly said "yes," I knew that a men's volume would become a reality. (Thank you, David!)

While the greatest gift, for the women in Volume 1, was the empowerment they got from sharing their stories, the men in Volume 2 were grateful for being allowed to be vulnerable:

*I am very grateful for your book because it has offered men a place to share their personal stories with the greater community. This is a rare offer and one that I hope continues to grow around the globe so that more and more people can see that men are heart centred beings too, and can be vulnerable. This is a new story about men.*

* * *

*It feels like a step into responsibility and accountability for me as a man to share my story with others. I want men to know how powerful, freeing, and 'manly' it is to feel and express one's emotions through life's journey. The world is a safer, more authentic, and more sacred place when men are empowered to share all of their heart with the world.*

I am so glad that I made the decision to produce a new volume of *Sharing* every year, and I am as blessed by the women in this, our third volume, as I have been by both the men and women in Volumes 1 and 2.

My vision, and my passion, were summed up well by a dear friend, whose words struck me to my core (Thank you, Cathy!):

*Your work is important, but it isn't work as much as it is a calling. It's a calling to bring together the power, the strength and the healing of others, so that they can be all that they can be.*

This is why I do what I do. I trust you will be as touched and inspired, by the stories in this book, as I have been.

Lisa Browning
Publisher

# House of Angels
## by Leilan Grace Adair

### Life's Treasures

*As you inspire the breath of the sea*
*Perfection is granted between you and me*
*Together we'll be incredibly wise*
*Bringing solace and peace to our everyday lives*
*Relaxing to the sounds and sights, we embrace*
*Each other, and the entire human race*
*Living is rhythmically challenging at times*
*But we are harmonic notes, forever in rhyme*
*Sitting quietly on the beach with the Sun warming us*
*There is gratitude for the bliss, effervescent in us*
*Leilan Grace Adair, Jan. 18th, 2004*

Dear Readers,

This account, based on our lives, and very real spiritual events, has deepened my resolve to live life—bigger. Fuller. Since my mother, Christine, was diagnosed with signs of dementia in 2012, the role of caregiver, for me, soared exponentially. A coach, born, on the run, in all facets of life! As for my mother, she remains committed to holding onto her dreams, freedom and independence. We are blessed with being on this ride together.

Writing and being published has been a dream of my mother's, as well as mine. There has been much fear, surrounding this desire to be published authors. In this story, House of Angels, we have shared with you a piece of our lives, to possibly, inspire you to step into your personal fear, make a change and bring your dream alive. It is with gratitude that I thank Lisa Browning for making my dream to be published, a reality! Thank you for guiding me every step of the way.

And to my friend, Crista Kundu, your feedback was beautifully timed. Together, we made the perfect triad.

Learning to manage, balance and live with our clair-gifts (clairaudience, clairvoyance, clairsentience and claircognizance) well, in this physically dominant world, would be another dream come true—for Christine and myself. We are grateful to our Reiki family and to so many other beautiful souls who have offered their expertise and helped us identify, decipher, and develop our gifts. With God, leading the way, our confidence grows, our fear diminishes, and blooms of empowerment, enrich our lives.

And finally, to our loved ones and friends who have stood by us through so many life changes, some easier than others. We are so fortunate to be loved and accepted for who we are. May you all be empowered with your own gifts of *Life's Treasures* and always feel loved and supported along your life's journey.

Blessing you with peace,
Leilan (ee'lon)

**Prologue**
**Toronto, 1956**

He was never coming back. Just as God had taken her father away, twelve years ago, he had been taken from his family and friends, one month, today. Only a teen herself, she had felt it, his death. Fear, grief and confusion had spread through her heart during their final goodbye. A dear friend of the family, Wolfe would no longer be visiting. A heart attack, on his way home from a visit with her family, claimed him. Christine sat bereft, in tears, on her bed; praying she hadn't been the one that had caused his death.

Thoughts swirled, incoherently, as she hugged her sweater closer. The cold she felt, in the middle of summer, was bone deep, relentless. Would she ever feel warm again?

2

A good man was gone. No amount of prayer had protected Wolfe from leaving this earth, as she had unwittingly predicted, weeks ago. Imagine, one hand shake, and the knowledge that family and friends would never again see his face, hear his voice, feel his joy for life.

She had done her best to dismiss, have the incident wiped out of her memory, but doubt and guilt had taken root. So instead, she grieved, fearful it was her wrongdoing that took Wolfe, just as she carried the sin of having been born. For in her mind, alone, she had caused her father's death.

Her father had been a good man, just like Wolfe. It was the end of WWII, when he had had a dream to secure a better life for himself and his growing family. A new home and job, in a nearby town, in southern Italy. She had heard the 'Il Destino—His Destiny,' story a thousand times, and she had blamed herself for his death, every single time. Christine had been the baby on the way, and in her mind, the reason for him not heeding his own dead mother's message to stay home on that fateful Friday. The same day that he saved hundreds of lives, he died in her much older brothers' arms.

She replayed the details of his death and how her mother had grieved, leaving her to be raised by mostly, her only sister, barely twelve, herself. Christine wept for them all. If she hadn't been conceived, he would not have felt the need to dream for a better home and a new way of life for her family.

Christine wept for her father, Wolfe, and for herself. How could she repent having had been born? And repent having had unexplainably 'known', it would be the last time she and her family would ever see Wolfe again? She had appreciated the elders in her family's attempts to accept that it had all been a coincidence. To let it go and move on. But she knew the truth.

She felt she had no other recourse; she had to suppress any similar 'knowing' feelings and hold all of it, hidden. She would be different, alone, but accepted--maybe, even normal. Done!

Suddenly, Christine knew that she was not alone. She didn't want to see it! Not another one! Christine grabbed her blankets and flung them up over her head. Paralyzed with fright, she shivered with desperation, hoping she would be spared further contact. And then, something or someone grazed the bottoms of her feet. Realization dawned, terror immediately rising. Kicking the blankets off, in a ninja fashion, she bolted, all the way to her Aunt Phil's and Uncle Rock's bedroom. Sandwiched in bed with her Aunt and Uncle, comfort and peace eventually enveloped her, a bit, and temporarily. The battle was not over. Somehow, she thought, she would be normal, her gifts buried deep. With a final prayer, she drifted into a light sleep.

\* \* \*

It was 2015 and Christine was still adamant about a lot of things. She would never go swimming in water higher than her waist. She loved her children and family immeasurably. And she would never say never to being re-married again. She would be at her daughter's wedding, one day soon, she hoped. And lastly, but most importantly, she hated the dark. This stemmed from her childhood. A secret only her family had known. But she had never let on the true reason for her fearing the dark.

She continued to worry about her daughter. Her son had his struggles too; but he was happily married with two beautiful children. He had found his life, in British Columbia, a long way away. And although she missed all of them fiercely, she knew they were safe and well. But Leilan, she thought, was stuck. "You are so beautiful, come here, give me a hug. You've got so much to offer. You need to have a life for yourself. You should just leave me. I'll be fine on my own." She considered herself a burden to her daughter.

Stepping back, Leilan straightened to her full height, five foot two inches and firmly stated, "You're beautiful too! And I am creating a life for myself! A healthier version. Just like you." Leilan gathered vegetables and fruits out of the fridge to juice. "But, you're no longer able to live on your own, mom. It's not safe."

4

Infuriated and frustrated, Christine hated being reminded of her memory loss, and limits. Her options had quickly dwindled over the last ten years. Her own symptoms of chronic fatigue, and fibromyalgia paled in comparison to the accelerated signs of dementia. She moved, misplaced and lost personal items and belongings regularly. She still couldn't figure out how she'd lost her assistive breathing mask. And Leilan had found her already replaced mouth guard in the kitchen sink's drain. She was hyper-stressed knowing that she played a big part to their financial stress, as well.

It was also becoming difficult to dress herself. Inside out, outside in, front or backwards. She paid no mind. At least she was covered. It amused her that she fit in with the latest craze of wearing different coloured socks. Looking down, she smirked. *Yup, one orange and one blue. No matter.* She shrugged, amusement distilled slowly back into disappointment.

She grimaced in memory of having acquiesced to wearing the medic alert bracelet Leilan had purchased two years ago. It had been a struggle, but this past year she had allowed the bracelet to remain on her left wrist, day and night. She wasn't pleased but knew it brought Leilan and her family some peace of mind. She rarely admitted to herself that she tended to get lost more often than not. The kindness of strangers had helped her find her daughter, many times. Her unabashed ability to ask questions and directions had been her saving grace on many excursions. And with the never-ending kindness of strangers, she felt safe, never lost.

* * *

The bedroom was black and suddenly her mom was beside her bed. "May I sleep with you tonight? Christine whispered. There's a man in my room and he just stares at me."

This was almost expected, Leilan thought, she shifted and turned back the covers. "Of course, mom. Get in and get comfy. We'll take care of this man together, okay?"

"Mom, did you ask the man if he had a message for you or if he was there to help you? If he was not there to be helpful or give you a positive supportive message, you demand that he go, and show no fear. You can also call on Archangel Michael for help. He'll take this Spirit back Home. Back to Love."

"No, I forgot everything. I don't know why he was there! I was too scared! The way he was looking at me made me uncomfortable and I ran out of my bedroom. I'm sorry. I am always forgetting. I'm not used to asking Spirits why they're here. As a kid, I just hid under the covers or jumped into bed with my Aunt Phil and Uncle Rock."

"That's okay mom. We can find out why he was here and see if we can find him. Maybe he is still around the building." She closed her eyes and scanned the perimeter of the building. He was outside their floor, searching for mom. Before she could tune in to ask him his purpose for being there, her mom says out loud, "He is a lost soul." Leilan thinks to herself, *Wow! You are powerful, like grandma! In fact, if she was going to help her mother, Leilan needed to step up her game, to be anywhere close to her mother's skills!*

"Perfect! Mom. Now let's both see the Light of God shining on him and call on the Angels of God to guide him home directly. No detours!" This made her smile. Leilan tuned in, once more, to ask if he had made it and heard, a thought from Spirit, in her mind saying, "He's gone. He's home."

Christine's face relaxed, as she quietly stated, "Thank you. I love you. I'll love you forever and always, no matter what happens." Settled once more, anxious facial creases relaxed, sleep quickly overwhelmed her mother.

* * *

She was sure she could let it go, and sleep, without any spirits waking her. Yet every time Christine fell asleep, flash back memories of her friend, Wolfe dying, after she had known that it would be the last time she would see him alive, haunted her. It was the main reason why she had chosen to shut down her intuitive 'gifts'; but they had still trickled in. She thought she had forgotten all of that, forged new memories of herself being 'clair-gifts' free but she realized now, this was not reality. She had to find a way to live in the now. And yet she continued to drift back. She turned her face into the pillow, anxiety and frustration reignited.

Memories of her childhood, and the unwanted visits from spirits began to flourish. The house, most of all, had been riddled with them entering her room and, sometimes, making themselves known outside during the day too! Though her Aunt Phil and Uncle Rock comforted her by allowing her to sleep between them, she never had felt completely safe.

* * *

Exhausted but gratified to see her comfortable and at peace, Leilan caressed her forehead as if to wipe away all of the nasty cobwebs away and whispered back, "I love you too." Squinting, the clock on the dresser read three am.

With her mother's eyes closed, already heavy with sleep, Leilan prayed to God, recited their 'House of Angels' prayer followed by a visualization she had created to help her mother see, feel, hear and know that the Angels were protecting them. Large and small ones. An angel filled every nook, crevice and cranny of their home. Windows and doors, guarded. Portals sealed. And Archangel Michael, on horseback with his shield and sword at the ready led his legions of angels, surrounding the building and neighbourhood. Leilan quietly affirmed,

"We love you Angels, thank you,
For protecting us and keeping us safe, always,
Surrendering to God's will, your grace
Fills us, with peace and security, leaving
Us holy space to dream, big!
And so it is…Amen"

Darkness enveloped them both, Leilan dared to hope that tonight's adventures were over even though there were still three hours until dawn. So until the fat lady sang her song, waking up refreshed and alert would likely remain elusive.

Cold seeped under the covers. Brain fogged and weary boned, Leilan scanned the bedroom. Her face went blank, disregarded completely by her mother. Sitting straight up in her bed, Christine spoke in serious hushed tones—to a spirit. Gosh, you really are dense! Leilan thought, as she propped herself up on her elbow, against the mattress. Mesmerised, she observed for a few seconds and mused, 'Why was she not surprised?' Leilan studied her mother, first with curiosity, and then shook off the enlightened moment with defeated exasperation. "Mom! She hissed, loudly. What are you doing?!"

"Shh!" She tossed back, her eyes sparked, briefly waiting to be challenged. Her mouth pursed with quiet disapproval. All signs of dementia long gone.

"Why aren't you sleeping? And who are you talking to?"

Nodding her support, to the unexpected visiting spirit, she ignored Leilan and continued onwards.

"Ugh." *Seriously! Five am. The clock was her enemy.* "Mom, you know you are going to be exhausted tomorrow. You need your sleep!"

The phrase, 'falling on deaf ears' surfaced in her mind, but no matter how irritated for her mother's and her own sleep having been interrupted, again, a huge smile pinned itself to Leilan's contented face. She'd remembered what to do and what to say for lost souls like she had taught her! A spiritual guidance counsellor had been born. A purpose, finally, and something she excelled at, too! *Thank goodness!* she thought. Now, to help her mother set and keep daytime hours for Spirits to abide by, instead of being counselled, all hours of the night. Leilan's mind whirled with ideas to make this a reality.

\* \* \*

Later that same morning, around 7:30 am, Christine met Leilan outside her bedroom dressed for a day at the gym. "Good Morning, dear." There was something about the way she looked. So tired. It made her nervous and a little anxious. Energetically bankrupt again, she supposed, a chronic exhaustion that called to her protective side. But her daughter was overprotective, with her, when it came to taking care of her needs and wants. When would she carve out a piece of this life for herself?

"Good morning, mom!" Leilan chirped, with a little more enthusiasm to offset the worry and concern she was covering up.

Christine laid her cheek on her hair and held firmly. Firmly because she seemed to need more strength. She had taken on a lot of responsibility to help her heal. A good grip was needed to help shore up whatever energy remained in her.

She could see her mother's own tiredness and gingerly asked, "Do you have anything to share with me about last night?"

Devoid of awareness, she shook her head. "No. Why, did something happen?" Christine automatically sought out, in her mind, what she had forgotten. Christine's solemn, warm brown eyes looked into mine and said, "Don't hold anything back from me." She held Leilan's hands and stiffened, barriers rising.

Leaning back a little, she shielded herself as bits of fear and pieces of anxiety slowly tumbled into place. Memories of last night's events erratically jerked out of her. They came, as quickly as they went. It was all so darned frustrating! "This has to stop, but how?"

"We will get through this together, mom. I believe you have a very good chance at having your memory back." Exactly how was another matter; but a plan was coming together, albeit slowly. The biggest twine to unravel was how to help her mother create healthy boundaries with spirits and people alike. Her mother did not know how to manage her spiritual gifts and Leilan was just learning herself.

She smiled, her eyes now twinkled, as she lifted a hand, and skimmed her fingers through her daughter's long, dark hair. "Guess who came to visit this morning?"

After last night's parade of unwelcomed guests, Leilan had no idea. "Who?" She only hoped it was someone helpful cause she was feeling overwhelmed.

"My mom and dad." She smiled broadly, contented.

"Grandma Immaculata and Grandpa Rocco? Together?" *That was a first,* she thought. *Wow!*

Christine nodded, affirming. Joy stamped in bold on her face. "They said something to me, but I don't remember." Disappointment and sadness zipped, fleetingly, across her face.

It was good to know that grandma and grandpa were lending their support. And this was the first time, they had visited together. "Share with me what you do recall. That will be enough." Holding her mother's hands, she listened intently.

"Well, I remember feeling both of their hands laying over top of my right hand. And I felt their words of comfort." Then disappointment settled, slightly, exasperation followed quickly. "I wish I could remember!"

"Mom! You remembered the most important part." She hugged her mother close and softly murmured. "They love you!"

**Epilogue**

Leilan had never expected to have this conversation with her dad, least of all, over the phone. Oh, she'd visited the thought of 'coming out' (dropped hints too!) about herself and her mother, with her father; but this time it had stuck. She struggled to relax, reminded herself to breathe. *Just focus. It's all going to be okay.* She replayed these words in her mind, repeatedly, until she heard her dad's familiar low, gravelly voice. "Hello?"

Keeping introductions brief, she jumped right in, fear and adrenaline embraced in the fall, "...Mom saw Grandma Amabelia while giving a Reiki session to me last night." Her breath caught in her chest. She waited.

"Did she say anything? And did your mother see your Grandpa Leo?" asked her father. He had imagined her shoulders tense and her forehead creased with worry. Suddenly he heard her breath escape in a rush, a sign of relief, he hoped. "Uhh, no and no." She took another deep breath and exhaled. "Grandma watched mom. Mom said that she could sense her curiosity about what mom was doing. But once Grandma knew I was fine, she left." Leilan continued "So, dad, I have something to tell you about me and mom. We tend to take on others' pain, emotions. Sometimes it's hard to distinguish where these feelings come from. Even emotional imprints can be left behind by people, animals, anything really, making it more of a challenge for us, at times." Silence ruled the phone line.

"I'm listening. Go on." She could see, in her mind, his studious face, concentrating, attentive. Her heart swelled, as she felt his heart open. His comments and queries held no judgement.

Woosh! Relief poured out of her, an inner smile, enveloped in gratitude. She had her breath back, steady and even, mostly. Leilan dove deeper into her mother's life with clairvoyance, clairaudience, claircognizance and clairsentience and then her own journey, milder in comparison; but still filled with some jaw-dropping episodes with Spirit.

Liberation had sprouted. Confidence had expanded, a touch. Authenticity, new. Now, she mused, *what would her brother say?* There was only one way to find out. She would pick up the phone, and start this same conversation, all over again.

\* \* \*

*Leilan (sounds like ee'lon) is a certified Usui Reiki Master and Reiki Instructor. She loves introducing people to energy adjusting and clearing modalities such as Reiki, Brain Chi, Crystal Therapy, Access Consciousness: The Bars and Body Processes (examples: MTVSS, Reciprocating Dimensionalities and Facelift), Axiatonal Alignment, and Shadow Energetics. She offers Distant Energy Clearing sessions, as well.*

*Leilan is working at the 'Inner-gy Centre' located within Healthy Foods & More in Waterloo, Ontario. The Inner-gy Centre will be open mid-November, 2015. Leilan is accepting clients for distant energy clearing sessions and booking in person sessions, on Saturdays, now. She can be reached at C# 226-972-8396 or email her at leilan.adair@yahoo.com.*

# The Very Hungry Caterpillar
## by Leah Frieday

When I was a child I was shown evil. I lived with its hot, sick breath relentlessly polluting the air around me. Even while the bad things were happening I somehow sensed that I would be okay. I only needed to survive the moment, just make it through until it was over. I grew despite those times, feeling that something was protecting my soul from being obliterated, but never having a religious or spiritual model I eventually lost that knowing completely. I never dared mention God to my family, or that I believed in something more for me, for them. It is because this belief was not nurtured that I began to understand the world as a place where only insidious things happened to little girls and that the evil of man was most powerful. That life is only what it is until it is over. I was 15 when I left home and began to destroy myself in order to kill the pain of my experiences. I was lost and left without hope.

When I met my husband at the age of 26, he brought a spiritual thought pattern back into my life. I began to see men as less evil and love as divine. Having him to talk to honestly and freely about God, I came back to the feeling I had sensed as a child. I began to feel that something was battling with me at my side. Within the past few years I have nurtured and fed this knowledge myself. I have a solid mind of calmness and assurance. I realize now that I had to come from where the evil slithered to truly believe in the magic of the universe. I had to know the devil intimately, so that I would believe wholly in what man calls God.

I witness and honour every moment of every instance where this intense power shines. Now, at this particular time in my life, I feel like it is roiling and bubbling inside, ready to overflow. I would humbly ask, if you will allow me dear reader, to have it flow out to you.

I have already begun to touch people in ways that I never thought I could. I know this is because I understand myself to be a link to or a tool of the divine. I have attracted through my belief in this cosmic power much more than that abused and abandoned little girl ever truly believed possible. I live my life for her. The tiny soul that sensed it could survive. I have never felt more confident, intelligent, beautiful, worthy and sure that I am on the right path. The thing that makes the "big girl" me excited, is that it has only now begun. Let me explain.

A few years ago my life was interrupted by an event that left me flipping from homicide to suicide. I discovered by accident, a brief affair that my husband had been hiding from me. It had been over for 6 months before the day I found out about it by reading an old email from him to her. Friday, November 10, 2006 at 2:06 p.m. was the exact moment that I thought my world had been destroyed. I share this with you because this day acts as the genesis of everything that I have become. And although it is hard to believe even now, it seems that this betrayal was the best thing that ever happened to me. Ultimately, this is how my spirit found its hum.

At first it took many hours, days and weeks to get my rage and devastation under control. It took months for me to resist packing my things every day and disappearing with his child before he got home from work. It has taken many nights of relentless tears and doubt, and almost a decade to get to a place where I am completely in love with my husband, my life, and myself. The reason I write about this 10 years later is that this is my most precious realization. In all of the ugliness I recognized the power that I could summon to lessen the rage and to ease the suffering, to forgive and love again. I understand that we all have a deep love to give, which is so much more than what the darkness can send. My life's work has become revealing this truth to others.

It took belief in myself, the devotion to my child and the fact that I actually did love this man to make me strong enough so that I could win this particular battle. In the moments where the vicious visions of the infidelity would come I stopped what I was doing and prayed, screaming for the universe to take the visions from me because they were killing me. My begging was lovingly answered. In these moments of mercy, I began to realize that this was my mission. That I needed to share with other people who are experiencing the same devastation, that they needed to see that there is hope of salvaging everything. That love, trust in a higher power and belief in yourself can truly conquer all.

In the end, it is not the actions we took to overcome this terrible thing…it is the belief that the endurance of our love is meant to be an example. That with constant reflection, meditation and energy put towards fortifying the dreams of our future, we will be who we are meant to be. We do not dwell on the past or live in a world of mistrust or suspicion. We create a world of light and promise, which we are shining on our daughter…this is the truest, deepest win for me. That she is growing and thriving in this light and that the cycles of my heritage have been fully broken. I feel my purpose in life has been shown to me and it fills me up beyond comparison to the affair that had once threatened to suck every last breath of love out of me. My purpose on earth is to help release the starving caterpillar and to help it transform.

I have been told that I have an extremely old soul…that I have been given specific tasks over and over, but have yet to complete them. I believe this. I also believe that bad things will always happen. I am not looking toward a life with the absence of negativity or problems. I look at it as if I intend to arm myself and others with methods and practices that will help deal when these things inevitably come along. I have witnessed the Karma truck dump its load in my front yard for things that I have done in the past when I was lost. It feels like, now, I have finally caught up and "paid the bill" and I am receiving all of the good things that are meant for me.

Through my beginning spiritual studies, I have been designated as a Master Spirit Life Coach, and of this I have kept silent. I became super protective of my calling after I encountered "Poop Preachers." It is so gravely important to recognize these people. Even if they don't say it to my face, it is the vibe they send out that can be a negative influence on what I am trying to do. So, for now, I am celebrating along the way with the people who believe in me; the others will have to wait and see. The biggest moment for me will be when someone says, Holy Cow! What happened to you?! Then I can say, have a seat my friend, let me tell you all about it!

My main message is that Love will empower you…love for self and for God, or the Universal power, whatever you choose to call it, should you choose to believe it exists. The evidence is all around us: in the way the sun sets and rises, in the way the atmosphere is made, in the way that the human body is created; all miraculous things that I can't consider to be mere accident. There must be a hand in all of this, a very good, caring, loving hand.

The fact that I am basing my coaching practice in Love and Spirit, and that I am on my own spiritual journey in becoming a Doctor of Metaphysics, means to me that this life will see my soul rest when my physical body runs out of steam. I have never been in such a state of growth, rebirth, healing, feeling, seeing…I have learned to accept and to forgive. I am learning that I can pick out the good things or "lessons" in a bad situation. I do trust that with faith, perseverance and hard work, I can become who I want to be and to achieve all that I am meant to. I feel like I am learning every day to be more in tune with the Universe, with the wholeness of everything and "the plan." They say the best way to make God laugh is to tell him your plans; I believe that there is a plan for all of us, much more than I could even conceive of… much more than any single human being on this earth at this moment could possibly see.

I see children consumed by ravenous predators of the innocent. I see young boys taking up arms against their fathers. I see mothers murdering their own flesh. I see babies starving because no food can be found, and I see young girls starving themselves despite the abundance. I see planes full of innocent people being employed as missiles. I see beliefs being used as poison. I see evil dressed as man. I see the human race at its weakest moment, but I know in the deepest depths of me that there is light and love despite what the world depicts to an observer.

*16*

The thing I rely on the most right now is that we, my husband and I, are being directed by a higher power to be beacons of hope in a world gone mad. We are constantly calling forth, conversing with through meditation, or visualizing this light that we have let surround us. I believe the conjuring of this light has actually protected me from becoming mentally, emotionally and physically ill, especially when I am around people that ooze negativity. If pressed to explain this light I would describe that it radiates around and from me with a purplish blue hue and comes from the place where I am hurt most…then shoots outward with fantastic intensity from that exact spot.

The fact that I am delving fully into spirituality as a profession is a bitter pill for many people to swallow. So much so that I have found it imperative that I shut down, or put aside, relationships that provide nothing but negativity, doubt, ridicule and even open hostility toward the path that I have uncovered. I can only hope that in my becoming, these people will return to me if they are meant to be with me. I have let go of the guilt of letting them go and have asked that they be shown the same light that was shone on me. The important thing for me is that the souls I come in contact with learn to believe there is something, a higher power, a bigger plan…and that by tapping into what is already in them, they can have their richest desires and their grandest dreams. You can have it any way you want.

Once, I had a belief that I could not be a singer. I knew I could sing, but the thought pattern was that I should have started when I was 20. I should take lessons. I should know how to read and write music. I am an almost 40, overweight housewife. I have a child and I don't have the right. Most of all, my appearance was at the forefront of the negativity.

One of the negative energies that I am constantly coming in contact with is this: You want to be a mother, a reacher , a singer, a wife…you don't have the time for all of that! I admit, there are some days that simply do not have enough hours for me to get done what I think I can. When this negativity bares its teeth I close my eyes and chant, everything is how it should be. This small meditative moment calms me and gives me the strength to keep going in the right direction without frustration or annoyance, or a sense of running out of time. Time is a gift we give to ourselves. It's not that people don't have the time; they just have the belief that there is not "enough" time. It all starts with the time you "give" to yourself…to sort things out and reenergize, and to turn up your own hum.

All this to say, I am accepting of the fact and thrilled by the chance that I have been given the ability to let this light shine in me and from me. I am being urged never to close a door and to knock more loudly when a door is slammed in my face. I have been given a voice and I feel the power. I will be led by it and help to lead others to it. This will be a neverending roller coaster ride of eliminating weakness and strengthening self-love.

I decided in 2009 that I would not listen to my negative self. I would let the world decide if I was meant to use singing as my method of nurturing others. I began to trust that all I had to do was put forward my best every time, and let the creativity flow out of me. When I did that it all started to fall into place. I believe that this is the way I have been given to reach out to and collect the kindred. I decided that the brutal discovery of, and recovery from, my husband's affair had wiped my own Karmic slate clean, and I proceeded to answer an ad on Craigslist for a singer/songwriter.

I would never have answered this ad had I not considered it a blatant kick in the ass in the right direction. I had never written a song in my life but, somehow, I knew I could. Of course, the opinions of my old demons had their say.

The only opinion that really counts is the opinion that you have of yourself…Nothing could be more true and nothing could be more difficult to alter. I have let go of what other people think of me. It has no effect on what I do with my life, or how my life unfolds.

But, then we get back to my opinion being the only one that really matters… What happens if you think you are soiled because of sexual abuse, you are not intelligent because of the lack of formal education, you are fat and ugly because you don't fit media's representations of beauty, you are too old to begin again, you are not worthy of being a mother, you are talentless compared to the rest of what is out there... you are less than because you have been cheated on? I could go on, but all this to say, these are the very specific, negative, dark black thoughts that were in my mind for the longest time, and I am only now being set free from them. It was easy to not care what people think; it is extremely difficult to let go of what you think of yourself.

The best way I can describe how I deal with my opinions of myself is this... Like a recovering alcoholic; day one you don't have a drink, which gets you to day two, where you don't have a drink, which will get you to the next day, where you don't have a drink... You never stop being an addict; you just learn to deal with it day by day. It's not to say that I still believe these things; my belief about myself has never been brighter, never more confident, never more full of hope and brightness...but, still, everyday, I encounter someone that wants to make me feel less than...or I may hit a wrong note, and think *Oh my God, and you want to be a Rock Star!?* I have allowed myself to acknowledge these thoughts, or the opinions of others, and that is where it ends...Thank you for sharing! Now, butt out! I have work to do and I have the gifts of the Universe to receive!

Visualization holds a high priority for me. This is where I rehearse for the songs I write, where I see myself with my daughter and husband in the future, where I decide and create what my spiritual mentoring practice will look like. I have stopped seeing a "too fat," "too old," "So you think you can sing?" housebound wife and mother when I look at myself. I now see a successful, purposeful, driven, healthy, happy, loving, caring woman who is ready to take on the world. I have been able to build up my own self-confidence, which feeds and grows from others hearing and appreciating my music. Through song, I aim to inspire others to live their dreams and to understand that love and abundance is theirs for the "making."

I will go on with what has been laid out before me, until I am physically stopped, or until I reach the goal I have set for myself...

*19*

knowing all the time that there will be another goal waiting in my back pocket to take the place of the present goal I have reached. Never stop dreaming, never stop believing, never stop learning, seeking, seeing... *that last line could quite possibly show up in my next set of lyrics!*

I feel that, in this reincarnation, my soul has never been closer to being at peace.

I'm reminded of *The Secret*...where they say that if you see life, or a goal, or challenge as a highway to your destination, with just the next 200 feet illuminated, you will get there. I absolutely believe in baby steps...therefore small pieces of the puzzle are being worked out...but the major, big picture goal is where my heart is set, where my aim is zoomed in on, Love fuels it all.

I have been steadily gathering good around me and letting go of bad. I have partners in this creation, for coaching in spirit and love, and the band I am creating with my musical soulmate, the man from the craigslist ad. I am working every day in the present, to manifest, to create, to work out what my job is in the now; at the same time expecting that it is all being worked out for me. Never for one moment forgetting to acknowledge, honour and luxuriate in the journey. To reach my destination and to not have enjoyed the road would mean total disrespect to the higher power, and an injustice to that little girl singing inside. It's important for me to be happy now, with the work part, the creative part, as well as the achievement.

My dreams are now in my husband's dreams at night. He woke this morning to tell me that he dreamed about seeing me on stage, singing one of my songs, and I was radiating with love and happiness. I have his energy, his vibe, attached to my dream now. It is so powerful, this feeling that we have of success. Almost daily, I see glimpses of who and how I will be in the future...like someone elbowing me saying look, look what is coming...like a preview almost. I am not letting anyone or anything get in my way of achieving my dreams. They are big...I admit that.... why dream small? I'm ready Universe....I'm ready!

I love myself as I am today. I can make better choices to become more in tune to this power that nourishes me and shows me who I am, who I will need to be and what I stand for. I am open to receiving what is meant for me. I have put no limitations on myself. I do not let others inhibit me. I do not let circumstances or the past dictate my thinking or my aspirations. I am witnessing the power of this primal, cosmic energy, every waking moment and even in my dreams. I hear the call. My eyes are focusing in to see the way, and I am open to the light that shines on my path. I see life as a myriad of beautiful colours, hues and tones, a melody and rhythm of love. I understand my creativity comes from a universal power, that I can tap into it, because it is a part of me. I look forward to my future with the eyes of a child, and the wisdom of the ages.

There is a door, a gateway, leading to a suit of armour that is available to us all. This is meant to shield us through the rest of our journey. I ask that you step over the threshold with great confidence believing that you are loved and protected. My wish is that I be allowed to act as the lightkeeper to this entrance for lost souls. I have always known that there was more to life than what was dealt to me. I have made peace with where I come from and with the people that have tried to bring me down, or tell me I can't. I hold no grudges; I hold only hope that they will see my light, and when they do that they will step out of their own shadow long enough to let it illuminate their path. I seek simply, to be a spark to their flame.

I want to spend the rest of my life surrounded by good people, positive thinkers, loving, caring, giving people. Most importantly, I want to be that person to others. I will never be bold enough to say I am evolved, but I am willing to shout out that I am evolving. I understand that finding my path in music and as a Metaphysician is accepting that I will be an eternal student. I have access to the tools, the wisdom, the great thinkers and doers…I want to play my part, throw it all in the pot. All of me, everything I stand for, believe in, truly feel, is a connection to something higher. I have come to shed my chrysalis…and love is guiding me to my destiny. Love and song, I believe, is how I will unfold my butterfly wings…and so it is.

*Leah S. Frieday, MSLC, CLC*
*Founder, Sacred Songstress International\* - Find Your Hum\**

*Leah's passion lies in assisting women to overcome the obstacles we all face daily, and to hinder the voices of the past from dictating our lives in the present. Together with a collective of healing muses and magical musicians, she shows us how to find our hum by providing the chance to write or rewrite the melody of our souls.*

# My Impossible Life
## by Charlene Jones

I stand in the red and white kitchen my mother painted. The cupboards have glass doors and my mother has pasted small decals of flowers —orange, yellow, white— on the bottom edge of each. She will slam those doors against their frame, screaming and slamming until the glass flies in all directions, the scattered shards of dark angels.

Not yet. Now she stands by the kitchen sink, her back to me, over the white porcelain. She talks to her budgie bird, "Pretty boy! Say it. Say "Pretty Boy." Tell me, come on now, who's a pretty boy?" She chirps like a bird, her voice sing song and the fowl, enchanted by my mother's sounds, encouraged by her sweet face, charmed by her warmth lands on her shoulder. It shoves its beak into its feathers, then hops on etch-a-sketch bird legs back and forth across her shoulder, dipping its head in rhythm to its own skinny sound, "Pretty boy, who's a pretty boy, achhhh."

I stand on a chair, just tall enough for my arms to reach up to the top of the round, white fridge. That's where the dirty yellow radio sits, its dials smiling at me. I am not allowed to touch.

In spite of this my fingers reach out. Without turning, my mother snaps her voice, "Don't touch that."

"I was just…"

"Don't. Leave it where it is."

Maybe it's Connie Francis telling me Everybody's Somebody's Fool, or Bobby Darin yearning for his Dream Lover, or the Platters, Only You. My small body rocks with the music I love. Sometimes when the Platters come crooning through, my mother sings, her voice pitch perfect and I feel her velvet. That's on the other days, when she may be making cookies, or peeling vegetables, her face smiling, her kind black- brown eyes suffused with love as she calls me, "honey." That is the heaven of my short life.

Not now. No softness now. Her voice bites the air and I hear the warning. Her voice is the first. The leather belt hangs at the top of the basement stairs to her right. That is hell.

Did my mother know? Did she ever see my brother's feral eyes peering at me, gloating with triumph after? Did she ever hear in his boy words the imperious humiliation he leveled at me, stripping me of emotional worth after he had invaded my body. For all her visionary ability I believe she was blind and deaf to him, her shining light.

Birthed from a line of Scottish visionaries my mother's mother, Gram, had been born with the caul on her face. Gram told me how her own visions began when she caught her waist length carrot red hair on the tracks of one of the first street cars, what she called a trolley, in Toronto. Outside the door of their convenience store my grandmother's screams pierced the air where the conductor slammed the brakes on, the smell of electricity acrid in his nostrils, relieved to see as he jumped down only the shining tresses of my grandmother's precious hair wound ever more tightly into his wheel, which had attempted and failed to pull my grandmother's head toward its demise and Mama, her one good eye trained on her only daughter, running with the scissors, clipped her daughter free.

My Great Grandmother, that Mama, stands behind her two small children in the picture from 1905. Taken when they first landed in the great New World, my Great Grandmother's one good eye stared down the present, peered through its veils into a future she found more tolerable the more she consumed the alcohol that fueled her blood.

Did he pluck the eye from her, that man, my biological Great Grandfather? His shadow seeps across the dock in Edinburgh where, toddlers in hand, surrounded by crates of silver cutlery, crystal vases, bowls, glasses, china the detritus of a marriage gone wrong, my Great Grandmother scans across the dangerous voyage before her to a land of safety.

Her Sight, and love of alcohol, ran true in my grandmother's blood, sang in her sleep all the nights of her life, whispering to her cells secrets of the future. I believe this because my mother had the Sight. I believe this because that knowing dances in my blood too.

Visions in dreams: as a child a single dream of horror returned three times: a green valley of slime. I want out! The first two times I scramble up the sides, driven by instinct to the top of the sides where I hoist myself up. Through broken concrete I look back and see the bloodied stumps of what remains of my legs.

The third time I have the dream I refuse that thrust and walk, terrified to the end of the valley. The dream tucked itself away in an inside pocket I didn't know I had.

It returned in the middle of the three days I was held hostage by two criminals, Al and Gary, who splayed a man's flesh to shreds with a sawed off shot gun, the smell of that blood fingering through my nostrils, flying back out through my mouth in bile and gorge.

"We're going out that door. You can run. The highway is 12 miles in that direction," Al's sneer twists his face, his finger points. "But we'll come after you."

"And shoot me dead."

"No," triumph in his voice, "No, we won't shoot you. We'll shoot the legs out from under you and leave you for the animals to eat." The dream springs out of hiding, green slime splashing across my inner vision.

That dream and the Angel I saw flying alongside the car where I sat in the back, the Angel come to tell me I would live. Later raped, tied to a chair, tortured, I was yet alive.

I had run away. At sixteen, I had run away from what looked like a warm, loving family. I returned, a hollowed out creature, secret scars on my body and deeper ones on the soul that shrank like a thief from everything.

So it was for the years I ran, drank, drugged, partied, worked sporadically, emptied my stomach contents into the always white porcelain bowl, was thrown like those contents out of the house, came crawling back on the tide of my parents' guilt and their attempt to rise above that with "conditions." What happened was I met a teacher, a meditation teacher.

I didn't like him. His contempt for the rest of us lesser beings fell all around, bits of hot charcoal from which we all withdrew. Then his mood changed and he drew us into his magical world of possibility, a potential he wrote in words across the air. He spoke and the world leapt with vitality and hope.

He left for a world tour in September accompanied by nearly one hundred student followers. It was 1972. I had spoken a promise to meet up with them, maybe in India, maybe elsewhere.

A vision: my small third floor living room after my night shift, my teacher saying, "Come now." I pulled on a cigarette, speaking out loud to no one, "I don't go half way around the world on the basis of no goddamned vision."

Within a week, a follower returned from Morocco where the group stayed, begged to see me and presented me with a one-way chance at England.

"The teacher," he explained, "told me when I left to tell anyone thinking of coming to 'Come now.'"

Six days later I traveled through India escorted by an elegant elderly woman with impeccable English, who served me tea and fed me fruit as the train chugged us slowly toward her home and my destination, Dehra Dun.

We arrived to the edge of the train, where a man pushed forward through the ubiquitous crowd of beggars. A few sharp words from him and they fell back, as one. In a moment her large black travel bags sat around a 1940's gangster style, black car.

"This is my driver," she explained to me and turning to him, said in English, "She will come with us."

His eyes twinkled merrily. He said, "Shall I give to the beggars?"

"Yes, yes, half a handful each." The handful of coins flipped through the air and some of the ragged, dirty flock scattered. About half remained hands outstretched, mouths moving.

"Go now!" he thundered at them and they all flew, tiny birds away. He opened the front passenger seat door for her and came to where I waited by the back door for a sign I might get in. To my surprise he opened my door, also.

Keyed up almost hyper alert, I slid in, fighting the urge to warn this kind, sweet Grandmother. I sensed alarm, danger in my body but put it off to nerves, the demands of the journey.

We pulled out of the station. They spoke softly together in the front seat. I was happy to be silent, anonymous, carried along in this great heavy vehicle. Out the windows this part of the country was green and lush in the way I recognized mountain terrain to be.

Suddenly the driver, his brown eyes piercing at me through their reflection in the rear-view mirror stated, "You are a very lucky woman."

Perplexed, I turned over different aspects of this. Then I smiled and said, "Yes, I am."

"Do you know," he continued, his eyes more intent on drilling me than reckoning with the road, "Neru? Do you know who Neru is?"

Great, I thought, 20 questions begun with politics. Try, try to think! "Uhm, wasn't he Prime Minister of India?"

"Yes, yes!" He was gleeful now. "Yes, and this is Madam Pandit, Neru's sister. She," he swiveled his head to reach his gaze directly at me, "is Number Two Lady in India. She is member of the UN."

Madam Pandit located the group, a five minute walk up the dirt road from her modest home.

Plunged into ten days of Tibetan Initiation ceremony at the newly constructed temple of His Holiness the Sakyapa, with no idea how sitting in a concrete room, sometimes for eight or ten hours, while monks threw water and rice around, flashed colorful cards in front of our eyes, wore red headbands and leapt about, while two Tibetans, one in colorful regalia, the other in simple robes, chanted and spoke, no idea how any of that would have any effect upon my life at all.

I had come because even I knew my home city held all the joys that continued to waste my days and nights: bars, music, drugs and men. I was there because I did not know where else to be, what else to do with this life. I was there because my feelings about life were simple: I didn't want it. Occasionally a tiny spiritual aspiration flickered off and on, a minute candle in the midnight storms of my unrepentant, undisciplined and self-indulgent psyche. In short I was desperate.

No sooner there than I craved return to that oblivion. I wrote letters begging everyone, especially my parents, to please help.

We flew into Australia over a sand sea of blood red sunrise. As the plane dipped down my mood rose: I was going home! Surely my parents, who had not spoken to me for those last days before I left but had driven me to the airport anyway, surely they would send a ticket. I felt certain.

My father's large scrawl on the very small pieces of paper he used, "Your mother is well…grandmother doing fine…new furniture here… dog happy…and oh, by the way, Buddha will provide. Get a job."

Rage, depression, tears, more rage, over the next six months in the worst heat wave in 100 years, rage and depression in the heart of Sydney's tenement slum called Ultimo. Various wanderers from our group straggled in, camped sometimes in the living room, bearing the flea infestation and oppressive heat long enough to arrange a move to more attractive places.

Six months, many stories later (slugs in the midnight kitchen of that slum, waitressing at a bar, brawls with customers) I had tried to meditate and failed. Repeatedly. Yet we boarded a ferry for the short ride to New Zealand and disembarked, heading for Blue Lake, the first of three settlements where our numbers began their intensive silent retreat.

Three months of silence, no TV, radio, letters, no phone calls and talking to a strict minimum within the houses we shared. Early morning each in her room sitting in meditation, rosary in hand, turning the beads over and over to mantras spilling from mouths while we tried to learn to visualize.

I got to 21 hours a day before the teacher told us to begin shortening our meditation hours. Did this save my life? Yes.

This and the many courses and adventures that followed: taking therapy in Mexico, then driving across to Cancun where five of us boarded a 22ft yacht, the Honey, sailing into the terrifying winds of tornado season; camping up the Norwegian coast to Finland; venturing through the whole of Italy into Israel where the teacher, dressed in camos and driving a jeep with three young men attracted the attention of the Government so we had to flee; renting every available Vespa in Chania, touring the island including the extraordinary Knossos; walking on glaciers; flying in a 4 seat Cessna; drinking chang with Mongol men until I recognized in the eyes of that young Tibetan woman who served us, a gulf of danger. I scuffed across the cliffs of life focused on a starry vision my head held, my feet barely touching ground.

In Mexico one morning my teacher had spoken about a dream he had had, one in which he was walking down some stone steps. Suddenly I could see the steps, covered in a bit of green moss, see clearly the image his words evoked, as though painted upon the air in the room where we sat.

"Yes, yes, that's it!" he exclaimed suddenly, his brown eyes lit with an inner fire turned on me. "That's it." I had visualized. And he knew it. My love of the mystery of dreams and visions opened in one moment, a moment shared.

When I finally touched down, when I stopped daring Life to catapult me into Death, it was to raise my son. His birth carved through my heart an opening targeting everything I had learned, felt, experienced, sowing it in veins of love and gratitude that began to blossom.

He was my motivation. I stumbled toward mothering, slowly, a large brute presence internally numb and awed by the tiny perfection before me. He was, he is the reason.

My teacher suggested I return to school, so I did. In 1985 I graduated with a double Master's Degree in Education and English. The Angels directed me back to Ontario.

I hauled my son across country and we settled in this cottage, our home, where I nursed my father through his last days.

In 1993 I decided to approach the Ontario Compensation for Victims of Criminal Activity. I needed external confirmation I had experienced the extremes. As part of the criteria, I had to see a psychiatrist. Upon hearing my story, he handed me Kleenex and declared, "With what you've been through, we'd expect you to be in and out of hospitals, under doctor's care for the rest of your life. You are not only functioning, you are high functioning. We don't know how you did this."

In the late 1990's I found a dream therapist and invoked consciously the languages of dream. I became a psychotherapist in private practice, specializing in dreams.

I have experienced deep trauma, yes, but all those long hours of those three days, my mother's imprint continued to speak. If I only endured the hell, I might find again a bit of heaven. Her imprint, the childhood dream that directed my responses to Al and Gary, Angels who refused to let me die, the insight and generosity of my teacher and my son as my heart's motivation fed me. My drive to be well, the extensive hours of meditation, dream contemplation, bio-energetics, breath work combined to push me through those doors of memory into a world of increased sunlight, of living in the present moment.

Currently my heart partner Harry and I live comfortably. My son and his laughing warm family are healthy. I host a radio show called Off the Top through Whistle Radio in Stouffville. My psychotherapy practice has continued for over 15 years. I have written two books of poetry, Bliss Pig and Uncritical Mass in Consort, with my poetry partners Linda Stitt and Cecilie Kwiat, a novel called The Stain, and am about to release a book on visualization meditation as explained by neuroscience called Medicine Buddha/Medicine Mind. Next year I will finish my memoirs called My Impossible Life. Neat title, right?

\* \* \*

*Charlene Diane Jones M.Ed/M.A is a psychotherapist in private practice. She teaches meditation based on her 45 years experience and practice with Tibetan Buddhism and her long explorations in Western mysteries. A poet, author, mother and grandmother Charlene is proud to be a member of Whistle Radio where she hosts "Off the Top" every second Tuesday at 3 pm. Join her to hear famous Canadian authors like Eva Stachniak and Tom Taylor, and others from around the world. Listen in to www.whistleradio.com every second Tuesday at 3pm. Go to her new website www.soulsciences.net where you can find her books and much more.*

# The Journey Back From Despair
## by Annie Kaszina

"When things got difficult, I just used to feel helpless, and give up," a client said to me recently. Larissa's words took me right back to my own roots... For a lot of years, despair was my regular destination, as it was Larissa's.

I was born into a very 'traditional' family – traditional in the sense that the man was The Head of the Family, the boys were apprentice Voices of Authority, and the women and girls were... second class citizens. It was never actually, put into words at all, but it didn't need to be. The message came through loud and clear that women were there just to care, serve, obey, and not compete.

I was encouraged to go to university – not because my family valued education; they didn't. But my father believed it would help me find a more prestigious husband. Like any sane young person, I desperately wanted to break the mold and have a different kind of marriage from my parents'. So, what did I do? I looked for someone who was NOT like my father.

Sadly, that didn't work out quite as planned. The trouble with being young and having to find your way is that you fondly imagine that rebellion will lead you to a very different place from the one where you started. In reality, rebellion is rather like a rubber band: sooner or later it pings you back to the kind of scenario you resisted.

How was I to know that when we're busy focusing on what we DON'T want, we don't do ourselves any favours? We don't have a clear idea of what we do want. So, we focus instead on getting the opposite of what we had – and hope for the best. My father was religious, so I opted for an atheist. My father was a businessman, so I chose a professional. My father didn't have a great line in conversation so I was attracted by someone who could – and did – talk for Britain; someone who was entranced by the sound of his own opinions.

Superficially, my husband and my father were very different characters. However, when it came to their beliefs about the care and treatment of women, they were remarkably similar. They disliked each other, a lot, but they shared the opinion that women were inferior, worth less.

What, you might wonder, attracted me to my husband? His sense of certainty, his belief that the whole world could be wrong but he was not, his conviction that he was a remarkable man. I hoped his certainty would shore up my wobbly sense of self.

In my years of working with many, many women who have – unawares – married their father (or, indeed, their mother) the attraction of the familiar has become all too obvious to me. You wouldn't willingly sign up to marrying the parent who drove you crazy, repeatedly disappointed you, or made you feel small, and yet... The sense of *knowing* that person, a certain powerful chemistry you feel, hooks you in.

At the unconscious level there's more going on as well: we want to salve the pain of not being loved in childhood as we needed to be loved. If we can make this partner-father-figure love and appreciate us the way we've always wanted to be loved, we'll finally be free of the past, and whole.

Needless to say, that didn't work out for me as it doesn't work out for other women who still carry their childhood hurts deep within. (Nor does it work for men in the same situation. I'm choosing to keep this narrative gender specific for the sake of simplicity and clarity.)

It wasn't long before I found myself fighting for appreciation and acknowledgement in my marriage as I had in my family of origin. Fighting in vain. That left me with two alternatives: either to foist blame on my husband – who I truly believed to be a superior being to me – or else blame myself. Since I was the common thread in these unfortunate relationships, and I was conditioned to live on the sharp end of family blame culture, I blamed myself.

Once again, nothing new there. That is what an awful lot of women do. We find ourselves in a relationship that we know is wrong. Our partner also knows that there is something profoundly wrong with it. However, since he lives with certainty, what's wrong can only derive from you. You end up with two people who both know there is something wrong. One accuses and judges, while the other defends and denies.

*Where do you go when you feel you've messed up the most important relationships in your life? When you feel unloved – and unlovable? When you feel worthless, and whatever sense you had of yourself as a person has vanished along the way? When you see yourself as a failure, and a no-hoper?*

I spent more years than I care to remember in that impasse. I wanted to leave but I'd invested too heavily in the relationship to go. Like Larissa, I'd given up on myself. Like Larissa, I felt that my situation was hopeless. Regardless of how long I might live, I truly believed my life was over. All the clichés about being broken and doomed to unhappiness, of being unable to ever recover and find love reverberated constantly in my brain.

Still, I finally left. Not because I expected things would get better. But I knew two things: first, I would die of misery if I stayed and, second, I was doing my child no good at all by allowing her to be a part of her parents' toxic relationship.

Needless to say, I did everything I could to shield her from the reality. But children, even very young children, are not deaf, blind, or stupid. We cannot hide our reality so thoroughly that they miss it. Children know their emotional habitat is unhealthy – even if they are incapable of formulating what they know. Whether or not they blame themselves, they learn some very damaging life lessons: at the very least, they learn to live in an unsafe environment, where anger and punishment can occur at any time, and love can always be withdrawn.

When I told my child that I was leaving, her reaction amazed me: "Thank goodness," she said. " If you hadn't, I'd have run away."

Does that mean that what followed was easy for her?

Absolutely not. Breaking free of a messy co-dependent relationship is never going to be easy for anyone concerned. Like so many other women in my situation, I had a massive burden of guilt to deal with – *because I couldn't give my child the childhood I wanted her to have.*

It took me a very long time to realize that I couldn't do the work of two parents, or take sole responsibility for the shortcomings of two parents. On a good day, I realized that I could do no more for my daughter than be the best that I was capable of being, keep the lines of communication open, and let her know she was safe and loved.

Doing my best for my child was relatively easily: even recognizing that I wasn't doing much good for myself took quite a while. Learning to treat myself with care and respect took longer still. The concept was completely and utterly alien to me.

My thought process was simply about doing everything I could for my daughter, and putting us on a secure financial footing. My own needs, and wants, could wait until everything else was running smoothly. I put myself on the back burner, for the foreseeable future.

I did know that I needed to heal. I realized I could have no quality of life if I was still caught up in the old dynamic of hurt, anger, and worthlessness. Forgiveness had to be the key to my happiness. I saw a psychotherapist to discover how I could forgive my abusive ex so I would be free to have a nice life. There were lots of people in my life at the time who thought I should forgive and – ideally – give the marriage another try. Or, if not give the marriage another try, at least get over it FAST.

Unless you've been there, you'd be surprised how uncomfortable most people feel when you tell them that about the seamy, sordid underside of your life. They really don't want to know. It's almost as if they fear your toxic relationship will be contagious. If they stick around you, their marriage will probably be the next one to disintegrate – not least because they know that you'll be unable to resist a burning desire to rip the much laundered underpants off their own dear spouses. So, all of a sudden, along with every other hurt and humiliation you're carrying, you find yourself unexpectedly ejected from the society of friends – lest you unleash nymphomaniac urges on their precious husbands.

To say it was a strange, dark – and sometimes farcical – time is putting it mildly. I ended up trying to be a curious composite of Super-nun (so as not to terrify my married women friends) Supermum (so my daughter wouldn't notice her father had dropped out of her life) and Super-saint (forgiving all the offences that had been done unto me).

Fortunately, the psychotherapist quickly dealt with my cozy Forgiveness fantasy. I don't think he used the word 'patronizing', but he did suggest I focus on my own issues instead of fixating on my soon to be ex *(even though my ex definitely had enough issues for two, all by himself!)*.

The psychotherapist's words led me to a group for women survivors of domestic violence, which is where my story, as a free woman, began. I learned about the dynamics of abusive relationships, and I learned that I wasn't alone. It hadn't happened to me because I was exceptionally stupid, or worthless. It had happened because, for my own reasons, I allowed the wrong guy too close to me; and because I had no sense whatever of self-preservation.

Like all of the women I've worked with over the last decade, I had an impressive – and ultimately self-harming – array of 'overdone strengths.' I was too selfless, too long-suffering, too committed to the relationship, too humble, too self-doubting, too generous-hearted, too naïve, too forgiving, too undemanding, and probably much else besides, for my own good. In short, because of my own issues, I'd been willing to settle for all the hurt and humiliation an emotionally abusive husband had dished out. It had caused me massive pain. And not just pain. It had led me to underachieve professionally. It had turned me into a hermit. It had destroyed my belief in myself, and it had shattered my memory. So much happened that I preferred to forget, but my memory refused to function in the highly selective way that I wanted. I ended up forgetting almost everything. Sometimes I wondered whether it was early onset Alzheimers. It was that bad.

Before I met my husband I'd always had a very good memory. The more I healed the hurt, the better my memory became. Even more curiously, my hearing also improved dramatically: it went, quite spontaneously, from poor to normal. I can only imagine that, because I really did not want to hear the cruel things my husband said, my ears stopped registering most of what happened around me.

Back in the good old days before I met my husband, I'd had quite a social conscience. As I sat, week after week, in the women's group, I became increasingly incensed at what had happened to all of us – and the emotional challenges we all still had as a result of the abusive treatment we had been through.

The received wisdom was that it would take a good two years before we started to feel better about ourselves. *Two more years of wasted life.* Not that the word 'healing' was ever mentioned. It was more a question of the unspoken assumption that it would take two years for our wounds to scar over, and for us to stop feeling unproductive and sorry for ourselves so we could get on with our lives.

That struck me as totally unacceptable. Because we had been hurt, humiliated and diminished – *in the privacy of our own homes* – we were a splendidly undemanding client group. There was no way we were ever going to agitate for the help we needed. If we could have done that, we wouldn't have ended up stuck in ghastly relationships in the first place.

I made a vow to myself that my healing journey was never going to be just about me. It was bad enough that I'd wasted long years of my life in a toxic marriage, lost out financially, and come to believe I was a basket case. I couldn't change that. But I could do everything in my power to ensure that other women rejected the abusive dynamic faster, and started to believe in themselves sooner, so they could build fulfilling lives, provide adequately for their children and themselves, and find loving partners next time around. My mission was to educate other women and spare them the pointless suffering of an abusive relationship.

At the time, it felt like walking a tight-rope: the only way I was going to be able to do it successfully was if I didn't look down, and didn't question my ability. Not easy, when you've had self-doubt drummed into you together with your mother's milk.

It was a scary time – and it was a beautiful time, because it was my opportunity to blossom. For the first time, I was free to choose my life, to decide what I wanted to learn, how I wanted to live, even who I wanted to be. I thought about going back into what I knew – which was secondary school teaching. It would have provided me with a stable income, but it would have consumed me. I wouldn't have had the time and energy to follow my passion and become the woman I hoped I could be. Teaching might have guaranteed my financial survival but it would never have allowed me to blossom. Stepping into my vocation, and the unknown, felt like a tremendous risk.

Over the years, I've listened to so many women who are in that dark place where I was then. They are almost paralyzed by the fear of how they can possibly cope without the man who has told them, time and time again, that they will never cope without him. That brainwashing has blinded them to who they are and what they're capable of. They tell me, without fail, that they are useless wastes of space. I listen to them, and then I start to tease out of them the gifts and talents they don't even know they have. You might be amazed by how remarkable ALL these women are. The women I've worked with – who believed they had no gifts and skills – have gone on to be writers and poets, they've painted beautiful pictures, become spiritual healers and wellness coaches, walked away from dead-end jobs and either created their own business or else found far better paid work. They've found work when they thought they couldn't get back into paid employment, found happiness when they didn't believe that was possible, and built lives they loved, when they'd thought that their lives were over.

Everyone who has ever been stuck in an abusive relationship functions on only a tiny fraction of their ability. They tell themselves a story about being on the scrap-heap when, in reality, they are at the start of the most joyous, rewarding, and successful period of their life. And this holds true whether they are 20, or 60+. When they ditch the old beliefs about why their lives are over, their world opens up in a thousand wonderful ways.

For myself, early in my life I'd wanted to write – but I didn't think I was good enough; or that I had anything to say. I'd wanted to make a difference – and had ended up as an outside caterer, making the most divine chocolate cakes. But that wasn't exactly meaningful – to me – in terms of making a contribution to the world.

Leaving my husband was the hardest thing I ever had to do. I honestly didn't expect to come through it whole and sane. Looking back, my only regret is staying as long as I did. Although I like to think that we stay as long as we do for a reason…

When I left was in many ways the perfect time for me. Many of the resources that were so helpful to me might not have been so available even a few years earlier.  I discovered newish modalities like NLP and EFT – which made a huge difference to my mindset. I found my voice and was able to reach out to women throughout the world via the Internet. Nobody ever wants to be a divorce statistic but, as these things go, I could hardly have chosen a better time; at least I was one of a very large number of women, and there was no social stigma left to being divorced.

In order to become the woman I am today, I've had to walk away from many, many things and places: I've walked away from my home and my county; I've walked away from my previous profession and my financial security; I've shed my identity as a daughter, sister, and wife. There has been a lot of loss – and there's been a massive amount of gain.

I found myself writing two books which have opened women's eyes to the unacceptability of emotionally abusive relationships. I hadn't intended to; those books just clamored to be written. I've been privileged to touch the lives of thousands of women throughout the English-speaking world, and help them blossom and grow. I've had a far richer life – and still look forward to a far richer life – than I would ever have had if I'd stuck with the bad marriage and the half-life that I had. I've acquired a ton of new skills and abilities because I was free to make my own choices.

Recently, I wrote a book I would never have imagined writing, "Do You Choose Your Dog More Carefully Than Your Husband?" It's become a multi-award winner. The frightened woman who didn't know how to 'do' relationships spent a lot of time working out what she was doing wrong, and how to change it. I now have a wonderful partner. My life is far happier than I ever imagined possible because I've learned the simple steps to creating a happy life from the inside out.

That's been my journey from despair to delight. It's a journey I never believed I could make. It's a journey I never believed I deserved. And it's a journey that's open to every woman: any woman can make that journey. It's not about believing in yourself, or being strong enough, or talented enough. No woman should ever let her internal dialogue about who she needs to be in order to take the next step get in her way. We women already have all the gifts we need. It's simply a question of taking one faltering step, and instead of listening to the little voice in your head that says: "Well, that didn't work too well!," taking the next step forward. All it takes for the miracle to happen is for you to take one wobbly step and then another. That's how babies do it. That's how a lot of late blooming adults do it, too.

Wherever you are now, whatever you tell yourself, if you haven't done it yet, you're still in time. You still can own your potential, and shine your light as the remarkable, gifted, precious human being that you truly are. The voice of negativity inside your own head has no idea of how amazing you are. Never ever believe it when tells you what you're not, and what you cannot be.

* * *

*Annie Kaszina, Ph.D, is a women's relationship coach, international speaker, and author of "The Woman You Want To Be", "Married To Mr Nasty" and "Do You Choose Your Dog More Carefully Than Your Husband?" She has spent 10+ years helping women to stop struggling with despair heartache, and self-doubt so they can enjoy the happiness, success, and fulfilment they deserve. Annie is passionate about sharing everything she has learned that makes a powerful difference, and has posted a wealth of valuable free resources on her websites:*

*www.recoverfromemotionalabuse.com*<br>*www.anniekaszina.com*<br>*www.ChooseYourMan.com*

*To connect with Annie, email annie@anniekaszina.com with the subject line: Personal*

# This Moment
### by Lisa Lindsay

I remember her smile. I remember her pulling me close as her body swayed uncontrollably, until our foreheads touched. I try to remind myself that I survived it.

I survived her suffering. I survived mine.

This story is about one of those events in life that you don't see coming. I felt blindsided by life. It is still an experience that is mine to hold. One that has helped to form me and that has changed who I am. An experience that has helped to reveal me, as vulnerable as it feels, to the world. I may not have wanted this to happen, but it has been a gift nonetheless.

I had been trying to connect with my mom one evening after having just been out to visit her the day before. I knew that something was up after I tried a few times with no answer. I dialed the superintendent of the building she lived in. She said that my mom had had a fall and had gone to the hospital by ambulance. After navigating phone numbers I was finally able to reach my mom in the Emergency Department, around 10:00pm that night. Her voice sounded almost childlike. She said that they had admitted her for mental health.

"But you fell," I said. "How are you? Are you hurt?"

"For mental health," she said clearly.

I said that I would see her in the morning and we hung up. I wanted to be there with her but I was exhausted. We had just had the funeral for my father-in-law a few days before and my dear aunt's was coming ahead in another week. I felt like I had nothing left to give. I would find out that that was not true. It was a story that I was telling myself. I could still give. I needed to.

My mom and I have always had an interesting relationship. She was a loving mother at times and at other times the symptoms of schizophrenia blurred that mom. I was a fearful daughter living with PTSD and a traumatic past. I let the stories of my past taint my present vision and maybe she did the same. There has always been love in the relationship, although mixed with duty and drama.

My husband and I arrived late the next morning after rush hour through Toronto. My mom was still in the ER. She happily introduced us by name to her security guard sitting at her door. She had been 'formed' when she came in for her fall. A form 42 is implemented for psychiatric reasons and prevents a person from leaving the hospital for 72 hours or until evaluated. We were told that security takes your belongings when formed so I went to retrieve them. There were none to be found. Her coat, purse and extensive bag of medications were gone. We were told to start our own search and that this was not their concern. As my husband began the search I stayed with mom waiting to hear what was to happen next. I didn't have the courage to bother any of the busy staff. I had been the same the day before when we took mom to see her doctor and voice our concerns about her pain and the changes we were seeing in her. I listened to the doctor rebuke my mom for calling the office everyday to say she was in pain. Scared, I said nothing. I will live with that now always.

Finally I had to find a nurse. Mom had been telling me that her left leg felt numb and now she had to go to the washroom, so I went to get help. I told the nurse about her numb leg and that a wheelchair might help. The nurse said that mom could do the walk down the hall. She appeared to be frustrated. I watched my mom walk down the hall braced by two nurses, her leg collapsing beneath her every few steps. Looking back, I am in awe of the strength my mom possessed. I always knew she was strong by the way she continued to live in faith and gratitude, no matter what she lost to her condition. Now I know her tolerance for physical pain and frustration too. She had the perseverance to go on even when no one would listen. Mom returned in tears. I asked her what had happened and she said that she fell again. (She had already had one fall in the hospital.) The nurse wouldn't look me in the eye. I stayed silent again and comforted my mom. The fear I had in this foreign space felt paralyzing. Who was I to be so anxious when it was mom who was so vulnerable and in pain?

As my husband searched for help with the stolen items he came upon an angel in nurse form. She not only guided us but listened to us. I pointed out that my mom came to the ER for a fall and pain but we were not sure if any test had been done. We had "fallen through the cracks" as she put it. Soon after we received the attention we'd been looking for. With this included the news that my mom's breast cancer was back. This time the cancer was in the bone. Why hadn't they taken tests before? These x-rays were done in response to the first fall that mom had in the ER that night. Exhausted and in shock I began making calls to get support for my mom's unknown length of stay at the hospital. At this point I was afraid to leave her side for fear that her pain would not be treated. More x-rays and an MRI were ordered.

After another long night my mom was moved to the oncology floor. Grateful to be leaving the ER, we had hopes for comfort and care, a new world with a new floor. Mom was being such a trooper. Although agitated she remained strong and grateful. She was now having short-term memory problems, bladder retention issues and a lost use of her leg (both due to compression in the spine caused by the tumours). A tumour and multiple fractures in different stages of healing were discovered in her shoulder (that she had been having pain in for months) and she had constant pain. She continued to have faith even with all of these conditions; the devastating news that cancer had returned and having not been heard by the medical community concerning her increasing pain. The strength my mom showed in a crisis always stunned me. When all the pain and tests invaded her at the hospital she always asked for the person's name and spoke to them using it and said thank you. Porters, nurses, cleaning staff, everyone. She never lost her faith.

For someone who judged herself and also was judged by others as anything but perfect, she was receiving an overwhelming situation with such grace.

A psychiatrist finally came and "unformed" my mom. He could not explain to us why my mom had been formed. His best guess was that it may have been to prevent her from having another fall if she went back home. We began to see the influence of mental health stigma on my mom's physical health journey. We had discovered while collecting mail for her that she had three invoices for ambulance trips. She had gone to the ER thirteen days prior, three times in one day to get her pain addressed. She was sent home the first two times with an education on how to take her medication, and the last time she left because she didn't continue to wait for someone to see her.

Next a doctor came in to say that the MRI was clear, no problems. Another opportunity presented to me to use my voice. This time I did.

"One hasn't been done yet," I said. As the doctor's tone changed the fear inside me began to flow. "It's clear," he said.

"We've been with her the whole time. X-rays were done and I signed forms to do an MRI but…"

The doctor argued that all was clear. I believed him, of course, against that little voice inside. I backtracked saying that "oh maybe some of the x-rays they took her for were actually the MRI." (I then began going to every test with my mom too). The next morning the doctor came in and sat down. "The MRI has not been done yet," he announced in a much softer voice than the day before. "Hopefully by Monday," he said. (Needless to say the results came back showing extensive cancer.)

Why is it that I will throw myself under the bus when someone gets angry, questions me or demands they are right? How was I to advocate for my mom if I couldn't stay strong and have enough faith in myself and my truth? I carried enough doubt in myself for a dozen people.

Over the next few days we came and went juggling mom's want for privacy, her tests, doctor visits and her rising anxiety with her new lack of memory when we left. Each day it broke my heart to remind her that she was in hospital because she had cancer. As we waited through more tests we were told she had about a year to live. They began radiation immediately in an attempt to get the use of her legs and bladder back. Each day we walked into this foreign environment that mom would be calling home for the next six weeks. We learned a lot about sitting with the unknown. We never knew how mom would be feeling, or when we would get to talk to a doctor or find out the answers we desperately wanted. We wanted to know what we were facing. Could we take a break? Could we go home and resume our lives for a couple of days? Our generous friends and neighbours helped us to make it through this time by helping to maintain our life back in our town while we lived this new life that we had been given.

We did go home for a weekend to get a taste of 'normal'. Our fantasy was broken on Sunday with a call from the hospital. Mom had a big drop in blood pressure and they were running some tests; not to worry, yet. We were already on the road back when a message was left on our voicemail by the doctor saying "Get here ASAP." Mom had extensive embolisms in her lungs and it didn't look good. We were told to stay the night as she might not survive it. Mom was unaware of the severity of her condition but was quite happy to have a sleepover and company for the night. I listened for her every breath that night. I finally did nod off and when I woke to see morning was officially here I knew we'd made it through.

Life is always about the moment. It is really all we have. We got the chance to live this truth moment by moment, even though in crisis we still felt grateful for it. We weren't lost in grocery lists or planning tomorrow, we only had now. She survived that night and two and a half more weeks. Time I will cherish forever. She did the dance of continuing to treat the cancer and not knowing if the embolisms would take her life at any moment.

As I adjusted to the unpredictability of my life, of mom's health and plain and simply each moment, I began to feel myself accepting what was. I call it my miracle now. I still can't explain what really happened. Mom and I have had our struggles. I wasn't the favourite child of the household. I had always felt a strong duty towards my mom though. I was not always patient. Being so sensitive I often ended up feeling hurt in our interactions. We had a moment like that in the hospital. I don't blame her as you lose all privacy living there. The sharp tone she used hit me. I prepared for the 'ouch'. It didn't matter. I realized I loved my mom and that my love was enough. I'd tried for so long to love in the right way so that it could be seen and understood. I wanted her to know that she was loved. I want everyone to know that they are loved. This time I just knew it was enough. With this acceptance it's like the past melted away, with all its pains included. The funny thing is it seemed to have happened for her too. It didn't make everything a rose garden. What I did feel was an acceptance. It was all acceptable and with that there was a peace present. We could be with each other and not in our stories of each other.  I became aware as our journey continued that I felt more connected with mom if I stayed in the moment. It was so easy for me to get lost in thoughts and what ifs. I desperately wanted some certainty to comfort me. Uncertainty became actually the only constant. In those moments that I was able to be still I could feel the peace that was already there, even with all the suffering and uncertainty, and that peace connected us. What a blessing. Forgiveness, acceptance, whatever the label it didn't matter. It was there in the moment taking me deeper into trust and into life.

I can't say it enough, how strong my mom was through it all. One night after the diagnosis of embolisms she stopped breathing. The nursing staff brought her back with a huge dose of oxygen. I could feel her anxiety and discombobulated state. Mom rode the wave through it all. She said that she wanted to fight the cancer as it gave her hope, so we finished the radiation treatments. I say we because I was her Power of Attorney. For a person who can barely decide what clothes to put on in the morning, I was now making decisions for the wellbeing of another person. I desperately wanted each decision to be exactly what mom would want, and I needed each one to be the right decision. The problem is there is no 'right' decision. The pressure of trying to convince myself that "I knew" what she wanted was suffocating. I did not know, and finally admitting that was freeing. I still don't know, and in every moment I remind myself that I can sit in uncertainty and can choose "not knowing" over sitting in pain.

We then pulled another all-nighter, the night mom received too much pain medication and her breathing slowed to five breaths a minute. They use a drug called Narcan to remedy these situations. I watched my mom return to us one more time. This time my heart ached for her having to come back. You could feel her travel back to us through deep layers of her peaceful rest. It really shook her.

We came in one morning to see mom in severe pain. This was the last time she was able to communicate with us verbally. Her condition still not understood; more tests were ordered. Finally, staff could agree on the term palliative. Once we were guided to the palliative floor we were taught about delirium. No one seemed to understand that this was happening on the oncology floor. By this point I was still trying to use my voice while balancing it with staying in the background as not to become 'that' family with staff. Once we were in palliative care things changed. I had the palliative doctor spend fifty minutes with me answering all my questions and explaining the process to me. This had been unheard of on our journey thus far. We prayed that things would be different in this department and that mom's pain would be seen and our prayers were answered. The night we arrived, we got the TV hooked up. My sister had said to mom that the hockey game was on and even in all her confusion mom excitedly said yes. Mom was a die hard fan. As soon as we turned the game on she smiled and calmed down. We trusted the staff immediately with her care and, leaving her in front of the game, my sister and I left the hospital for a bite of dinner at the same time, for the first time in weeks.

As our journey continued I reminded myself over and over to be here now with her. Now is all we have. As we started our advocacy work on behalf of mom it was easy to get pulled into collecting notes and timelines for investigations. They wanted to sedate mom as they said delirium was actually stressful and she was suffering. I went to mom to say "I love you" and to ask and give forgiveness. Weaving side to side she brought herself forward. She brought her forehead to mine and we sat, foreheads kissing. This memory is a gift I will always carry with me. A chance to say goodbye. A chance to be with my mom and mom with me, one last time.

I slept overnight in the palliative unit in style, with my very own cot. My husband had his own beside me. During the second night I awoke and got up to swab my mom's mouth around 3:00am. I read a page from Joan Halifax's book, Being with Dying. I saw how I was holding onto mom as 'mine' and I was reminded that mom was not alone in her suffering. It was not her suffering or mine, just suffering. This allowed me to re-centre and brought tremendous peace. I nodded off. Around 3:45am I jumped out of bed. I still have no idea how I knew to wake up. I believe God tapped me on the shoulder. I recognized instantly that mom's breathing had changed. She was leaving us. I held her hand and focused with all of myself on being present and there for her on her journey. Then Mom was gone. I could feel her in the room still, but she felt unfamiliar to me. I had been there with my aunt when she died a month earlier. I could feel her too in her room when it happened. It felt like a vast spacious version of my aunt. I see now it was a grace-filled mom but, with all the suffering removed, she felt unfamiliar to me.

When we finally got back to her apartment that morning with much to plan and accomplish that day, I sat down trying to catch up with life and all that had happened. I suddenly felt mom so clearly, nothing to doubt myself with this time. "I'm okay now." Even now I can remember this so clearly, and the feeling of it. I hold onto this when the grief feels too much to bear. This moment just happened. I didn't try for it or control it into being. It happened.

I have learned that freedom, even power, isn't having things go a certain way, my way. The peace and presence I want is here and now. This doesn't mean that I didn't share our story with the hospital and question her physician. It means that I attempted to come from presence in doing so, not searching for peace with her death in an outcome or in investigations. From childhood I have feared the unpredictability of people and of life. I have experienced on this recent journey that in fearing the unknown and the mystery of life I can still keep my heart open to it all, even in the hardest of circumstances. I can be vulnerable and survive. I can use my voice and still survive. There is so much that I have left out of this story. What isn't missing for me is the feeling of aliveness and of love. In reliving this as I write, I can feel the healing. I can feel the pain. I feel the loss. I can make room for it all. Now, months after this journey, with investigations almost complete, I am getting to grieve. I tightened my open heart as I came back into my life routine and tried to meet the demands of life. I look back and see what I was able to accept and be with, and can't help but hope that maybe I have inherited just a little bit of the strength, faith and gratitude that got mom through it all. In finding my voice I have seen the humanness that forms the medical system. With compassion I can say that they make mistakes too. I also see that they are not the intimidating authority that I once let them be in my life.

I have called upon that strength in order to write this and tell my mom's story in hopes that it may help others to find their voices, particularly in the medical system, should it ever be needed. I can hold my suffering, be witness to it, and help hold others suffering and still survive. And even continue to love. I now see that being vulnerable is powerful. I have judged it harshly in the past. In accepting what is, we are vulnerable in every moment. Allowing vulnerability is definitely scary for me, but it has also empowered me to truly live.

* * *

*Lisa Lindsay lives in Guelph. She is continuing her grief journey and living more deeply with each step. She wrote this in memory of her mother. "Death is not extinguishing the light, it is only putting out the lamp because the dawn has come". Rabindranath Tagore*

*I love you mom.*

# Don't Be Fooled
## by Deb Maybury

*It was a chilly winter morning in Kapuskasing, a northern Ontario community, when I became mesmerized by an ice-coated meter box attached to the back of our bungalow. I had seen it shining many times, but it had never captivated and lured me as it did at that moment. Without hesitation, or concern, I marched toward the appealing delicacy, stuck out my five year old unsuspecting tongue, and took one anticipatory sweep. Consider my horror when I became latched to the over-sized Popsicle - I was literally, painfully, frozen in fear. I have no subsequent memory of that event and hesitate to even consider what I endured to release myself.*

The wisdom of the mind is often beyond our awareness, and intellectual ability, to comprehend. It knows how to keep us alive, how to protect us and allows only what we can manage, at any given time, into full consciousness. Those experiences are subsequently filtered through our coping strategies, which are often numbing and self-sabotaging. We are left with the various masks we wear – not to mention our outlook on life. The mere fact that most people survive childhood commends our ability to adapt.

My childhood was complicated, harsh or interesting – depending on your perspective. I was navigating in a maze, not knowing I should probably consider looking for an exit sign. Early memories include being alone a lot, feeling very different than everyone in my family, my parents yelling, being told we were going on a holiday and never returning home, dad's affair, my parents divorcing, experiencing little affection, being left with in-laws while my determined mother went to school or worked, a wonderful but absent father, alcoholic family members, a *do not talk about feelings* unspoken rule, few friends and enough other convoluted matters to fill a book. Fortunately, I was blessed with an innate ability to deflect and/or integrate a lot of *stuff*, some invaluable resiliency and angelic people that randomly appeared.

Notwithstanding my youthful adaptability, I was rocked by a shady series of events beginning shortly after my parent's separation – between the ages of six and ten. Some forty plus years later, I can vividly recall every scene, feeling and thought of being sexually violated by a handful of persistent predators. Every face and name is etched in my mind, as are the words they professed in order to groom my trust and deplete my innocence. The mystery boy in the public pool, which was bursting with excited and naïve children, comes to mind just now. He attempted to persuade me to allow him to navigate his hand either up or down my one piece bathing suit. A teenage pedophile pursuing an unattended little girl – a soon to be savvy, predator-avoidance little girl. He, like all of them, tried to convince me I would enjoy what he sought. I understood exactly what he was proposing and I did *not* enjoy *it*. I evaded his advances by declaring that his hand, not to mention his self-absorbed entitlement mentality, was too big to fit under my bathing suit.

During those early years, it seemed like it didn't matter where I was, I was a target for unwanted and very confusing *touchy* attention. Ironic, in a sense, because I yearned for healthy attention and affection – which to me was a hug, playing, or someone actually interested in me and what I was doing. This is so typical of children that are sexually violated. They lack healthy physical and non-physical companionship, and the pedophile detects that absence and fills the void. He/she actively and skillfully builds trust with the child, and often his/her parents, which ultimately earns them isolated time to violate the child.

I was repeatedly tricked to believe that my perpetrators were *playmates* – who happened to be older. All but one were teenagers I knew and trusted – no one would have suspected them. At one time they had been perfectly safe and fun to be with. They were too old, and I was too young, to excuse their behaviour as *playing doctor*. I remember our encounters changing, from what I understood to what was confusing, and from me actively playing to freezing. This was palpable when the perpetrator turned into a sometimes babysitter male friend of my mothers. I was ten, he was forty-two. I continued to say a firm "No" in my mind, yet remained silent and unable to articulate my thoughts.

*Alan* and my mother had known each other years prior to his resurfacing. They were friends, then dated, then returned to just friend status. Typical pedophile behaviour – find a single woman with children. He was eerily charming and attentive around my older brother and I. He took us fishing, camping and boating, among other things kids are drawn toward. I admit, at first, I liked him. He was interested in everything we did. He rewarded our athleticism with money and toys. Then, one night when my brother went to bed early, he crossed the line while we were watching television. At first I wanted to forget and go back to him being a *good guy.* But when his actions continued to demonstrate that he wasn't a good guy, I accepted that, and decided *never again, no more.* It didn't take long for me to deeply hate him. I decided I wouldn't be where he could violate me. I was successful for a while but I wasn't as smart, or as devious, as he.

I was terribly upset at myself when I trusted him and got into his car. (This encounter is written in my compilation book, *Unlock The Door – Beyond Sexual Abuse.*) I would not unlock the car door so he could take me into his apartment. He manipulated me and we ended up parked in his driveway. I remember the sick frightening feeling when the car turned toward his place rather than the store. Too often parents think they have soundly educated their child and he/she would never go with a predator; they are wrong. A pedophile knows how to lure a child very quickly. It's not the stranger you typically need to be concerned about, it's the strange behaviour you must always be diligent to notice and disclose, whether or not you know the person. I demonstrate our failure to teach this lesson repeatedly when I teach self-defense to teenage girls and women. I create a casual conversation with the group and then select a volunteer. I ask her a series of questions and it takes several questions before she realizes she is being set up. I ask who she lives with, where they live, if there are children home alone after school etc. After establishing rapport and a minuscule amount of trust, I am told everything I ask. We are very trusting creatures by nature and children are helplessly unsuspecting and vulnerable. I was mindful and I was tricked.

My stomach turned as I watched Alan get out the car with the expectation I would follow him – wrong! He attempted to negotiate to no avail. "Debbie, unlock the door." I miraculously got out of that situation, traumatized yet untouched. I was no longer the same child when he took me home after realizing I was no longer his accommodating puppet. That afternoon, it was forever engrained – there were things I couldn't control and things I could. I recognized I must take control and never let my guard down again. I was ten and knew I was not only responsible for my own safety, but I could take care of myself. I was so mad at him for deceiving me – but, he got the message.  No more. Ultimately, I felt I had craftily outsmarted him by locking the door and pretending my defiance was a game. He abruptly vanished, permanently, out of the picture. Even though he had taken me home and said he wouldn't do *that* again, I wished him dead over and over. Strangely enough, on the positive side – that incident helped me gain a good deal of confidence. However, on the not so positive side – I felt alone and every creek on the floor, noise at my window and taxi cab churned my senses.

I continued to feel like a magnet and needed to figure out how to break free from the *sickos*. I reiterated, to myself, that I would never again be touched inappropriately. When you are young there are only a handful of options. Telling was not an option. I did not know how to do that. I did the only thing I could – I recoiled. I isolated. I did not seek to be alone with anyone except people who had already sincerely earned my trust. There were a limited number of them outside of my immediate family. I couldn't take a chance. Where I once sought attention I stopped. I even began feeling embarrassed when attention was innocently placed on me.

Most of my non-school time was spent alone or playing sports. I started to be called shy but I had simply become private, vigilant and cautious about my personal space. I didn't talk a lot, unless called upon, because I didn't trust or even know how to like someone new without feeling a little uncomfortable. I developed the attitude that crap was part of my life – but I didn't have to show up or tolerate all of it. I had endured enough from others, so I decided to do my own things. I proceeded with my new attitude, and the sexual violations ceased.

Trauma affects everyone in a unique and unpredictable way. Memories from my sexual violations have never haunted me viciously as nightmares or reoccurring flashbacks. (The exception being the night I conceived *Unlock The Door – Beyond Sexual Abuse*, when the memories were relentless until I got out of bed and wrote about the driveway incident.) When I place my attention on the experiences, they appear; when I don't, they seldom intrude. I am fortunate that most aspects of the abuse seem to have been contained without much conscious effort. I have not suffered to the degree of others and will be forever grateful that my recollections are dirty memories versus strangling unforgiving ones.

Do not be fooled; I am not without my wounds. I suppressed a good measure of hatred, anger and sadness, among other things, due to the actions of perpetrators and the non-action of adults I felt should have detected the mountains of evidence and rescued me. Only recently it dawned on me that they may have suspected and I was oblivious to it. I say this because when I noticeably separated myself from certain people my behaviour was never questioned. I was never *made* to spend time with any of them. Maybe my caregivers had a sense of what I was exposed to yet did not want to draw attention to it or discuss the circumstances. If I said, "I don't want her as a babysitter," she was gone; "I don't want to go there," I wasn't forced to go.

As time distanced me from a turbulent childhood, and the fantasy that my childhood vacation would conclude and I would finally be returning to life in Kapuskasing, I continually filled my schedule and focused on creating more appealing memories. I self-concluded that the past was the past and I simply attempted to not think about the difficult times behind me. I escaped into my adult version of make-believe – a life of creativity including writing, painting, graphics, sports and eventually entrepreneurship. That was where my heart danced and my inner discomfort was undetected. I left home, entered a long-term relationship, drifted through university, excelled at ice hockey (playing in the First Women's World Tournament in 1987, becoming the first woman to referee at the First Woman's International Ice Hockey Championship in 1990 and coaching at York University for a few years), co-established a graphic apparel business (currently in its 26th year) and diligently studying martial arts and fitness.

The years flew by and though I was creating an interesting life, my old life was slowly re-emerging. As my mid to late thirties rolled around I had a wakeup call. The doctor discovered a fibroid in my uterus, the size of a cantaloupe. I knew enough to know that my childhood emotions and experiences had found a secure place to reside. I had not forgotten; I had merely suppressed the memories which had been confusing and hurtful. Tolerating the past was no longer working for me. Even though my *keeping busy coping strategy* had been less evasive than, for example, numbing techniques such as drugs, alcohol, eating disorders, cutting and depression, I was still hiding from a part of me and I felt non-authentic. I distinctly remember being at martial arts and watching my closest peers and feeling distant and unconnected – yet bonded, if that makes any sense. I didn't really understand what I was feeling, but once I acquired this new awareness I could not go back into unknowingness. In an attempt to actively acknowledge and release the past, I started to tell myself I forgave all the people that had violated me.

By the time forty arrived, circumstances persistently beckoned me to speak out. After a lot of contemplation I chose to acknowledge the violations when the right opportunity emerged. That happened while teaching a self-defense class at a high school. A teenager asked why I taught women how to protect themselves, ("and Miss, did something happen to you?") and in a moment of truth I said, "Yes, when I was a young girl I was sexually violated." I was no longer hiding. I felt vulnerable, but damn it felt so honest and raw! A weight was lifted and I found the voice I'd lost.

I quickly discovered I was neither alone nor unique. It was uplifting to know that my acknowledgement permitted many women to reveal their abuse to me and release their sense of isolation. Most women and men sexually victimized in childhood do not reveal the abuse. They were/are shamed and guilt-ridden unmercifully into silence, they begin to tell and are hushed, or think their admission will negatively affect how they are perceived and treated. We are not taught vulnerability is a strength, so we hesitate to be forthcoming. Though I never thought I had done anything wrong regarding the sexual abuse, I was silent, mostly because I felt I would be defined and judged by it. I was horrified to think that someone would put me in the cycle of abuse and think I might partake – it makes me feel sick to even acknowledge that closeted fear.

Disclosing sexual abuse is not easy. I anticipated mixed receptivity and proceeded delicately experimenting how best to share. I proposed what happens to us does not have to define who we are. I am not the abuse, my adoption, my parents' multiple divorces or a host of other challenges; I am me. It became increasingly important to share my message while teaching martial arts, giving seminars, and whenever the topic came up. My first attempt to write under the umbrella of my message came in 2008. I heard a local high school teacher I knew had been charged with sexual offences against a girl that attended the very high school I was on my way to that day. He was a 52 year old gym teacher; she an 18 year old student. By the time I got back to work I had the idea to write *What Is Your Teenage Daughter Afraid Of?* I surveyed hundreds of high school girls and asked what they were afraid of. The number one fear? Being sexually violated. That research was very enlightening and another piece of my puzzle.

As an adult I am responsible for shifting my coping strategies, perceptions, and community to reflect who I chose to be. I once thought, like every abused child, that I was the only kid being violated. Why me?! I thought maybe something was wrong with me that attracted the *sickos*. I wasn't wise enough to realize I was one of many children in similar situations who were at the wrong place at the wrong time, with people who took advantage of kids needing attention. (Not to mention all the children within their own homes being sexually abused.) I had no voice and a short list of options. I did the best I could with what I knew at the time, and in my forties that knowledge was about to multiply rapidly.

As I continued collecting black belts, real estate and a history of broken relationships, I began searching for the *real* Deborah Maybury.

One of my original Kung Fu Masters asked me to assist him at a personal growth event in Calgary, back in 2003. That event lead to several others and changed my path by vaulting me onto a journey of self-discovery. Since then I have participated in sweat lodges, fire walks, rebirthing, trace dances , silent retreats, and even found time to cycle across Canada, in the Sears National Kids Cancer Ride, in 2010.

Around this time I also revisited the topic of forgiveness. I had to be honest. I had been telling myself I forgave everyone for their violations. It wasn't true; I hated them all. When I pictured Alan in front of me, to see if I forgave him, I kicked him with the enthusiasm of years of martial arts training – so hard in fact that I imagined him choking on his seminal fluid. (Sorry about the visualization, but that was the extent of my disgust.) After finding some humour in my false forgiveness I began focusing on the fact that I'd had a right to be angry and I had developed several, both positive and not so positive, characteristics because of my past – I was okay overall with who I was becoming. Believing I must forgive, to heal and move on, seemed erroneous. In fact, what I discovered is that many survivors of abuse attribute the inability to forgive as a further burden and trauma. So, I let go of forgiveness, it's a non-issue for me – unnecessary. Everyone is entitled to their belief and, as long as it promotes self-love, I support it. It may be semantics, but I use the term *accept*. I can't change the past. I can only change my perspective and how I integrate what happened into a part of me that flows and serves. The truth is, I wouldn't change the past if there was an option to, so forgiveness is unnecessary – a moot point. I don't condone their behaviour, nor wish what I experienced on anyone; I simply know if I change my past I change me … and I like the imperfect me; she's still doing her best and forging her own path.

Shortly after the high then low of the Sears National Kids Cancer Ride across Canada, my brain felt too busy with everything. I felt I needed to refocus and/or somehow escape. It was driving me a little crazy not knowing how everything I'd done was meant to fit together. I knew there was something big on the horizon because I'd had a vision as a child. (That's a long story – maybe one I'll share in another book one day.) It was November 2011. I had completed my goals for the year and lay awake in bed asking, "What's all of this about?" I was ready to make sense of my life and to learn the purpose of everything up to that moment. I was diligent and repeated the question over and over again until the sexual abuse memories hit me erratically like never before. My attempts to push them aside vehemently failed. I was compelled to get up and write my story – I cried and cried uncontrollably throughout the writing. More accurately - I *bawled* nonstop. That had never happened – ever! Everything came out. It was both cleansing and confusing.

I went back to bed and proceeded to ask "WHY" those memories had surfaced. The response I received was, "Write a compilation book (*Unlock the Door – Beyond Sexual Abuse*) and be the messenger for all those people who cannot speak." Everything in my life led up to that moment. *Unlock The Door* was the single most difficult thing I have ever done. It was a beautiful eighteen month marathon of reading, researching, interviewing, connecting and healing. I entered group therapy to make sure I was okay. Then I continued (almost four years now) to facilitate groups at The Gatehouse. The Gatehouse is a safe place, for people who have been sexually violated in childhood, to share and learn. As I finish this chapter I am thinking about a speech I have to give tomorrow at York University, about sexual abuse recovery, and a psychotherapy assignment I have to finish. My life is immersed and focused on helping people heal and recover. It feels like everything has come full circle.

In conclusion, there are two things I want to share.

I've had several angelic souls appear at critical times who guided me with their wisdom and actions. We all make a difference in someone's life – whether we think so or not. Two of these special people touched me deeply when I was a lost teenager. They never realized their impact on my perception of myself and life. They are two of my greatest gifts.

Mr. Gordon Nichols was my grade eight teacher. I think he sensed my shyness was a facade. He selected me to act out both *Please Wear A*

*Poppy,* for the Remembrance Day school assembly, and Mrs. Santa Claus in the Christmas school play – which was also performed at the local Kingston Women's Penitentiary. On Friday afternoons we would have *Fun Friday* and discuss the deeper meanings of songs and plays, and he would make us share something personal then everybody would repeat, "I'm okay, you're okay, we're all okay." He gifted me confidence and a different way of thinking while removing a couple of bricks in my thick wall.

Mrs. Donna Mohan was the mom of a teammate. I rode with their family to games and tournaments. At one tournament I was deathly ill and she took me to the hotel to rest after a game, then went with the team to dinner. As I lay there half asleep I heard the door open and she said, "It's just me" very softly. As I lightly opened my eyes I saw her place an apple, muffin and bottle of ginger ale on the bed stand. She said, "These are for you; try to eat if you can" as she touched my shoulder. As she turned to leave she said they'd all be back soon. I felt tears emerge and threaten to escape onto my cheeks. I squeezed but failed to control them in. Her gesture suggested I mattered – she really cared. She didn't have to bring me anything; certainly it could have waited until later. It hit me squarely in my heart. I felt loved. I got it – some people can really show they care. I learned that little actions can be powerful guides. She emitted a warmth that radiated and I hope somehow I can share, even a fraction, of what she gifted me.

**One encounter can change a life.**
**Share your story, be vulnerable and make a difference.**

\* \* \*

*Deb Maybury is an entrepreneur, author, speaker, musician, facilitator and advocate who specializes in sexual abuse recovery and helping people realize and share their unique gifts. Please visit her website at www.debmaybury.com.*

# Loving My Curves ~ Recovery in Progress
## by Kimmy Murphy

Okay, you caught me. I am so not in love with my curves. But the difference between me now and me from before is that I want to be. I'm working towards loving myself inside and out.

I started out like many teenage girls, not really comfortable in my own skin and simultaneously dreading and looking forward to high school. I had never had a boyfriend and most of the guys I knew regarded me as one of their own. And I was a little sensitive about my looks from having been teased about horribly crooked teeth and being excessively hairy. I felt slightly more confident starting high school after a summer of getting acquainted with wax hair removal and a retainer. As the first year wore on, guys still weren't asking me out and I lost my confidence. At age 14 it was extremely important to feel pretty and have a boyfriend. If only I could take my 14-year-old self aside and show her the bigger picture of life.

In the spring, a guy noticed me. Finally! He thought I was gorgeous and worshipped the ground I walked on. I was in love with being in love. So much so, that I cut off all ties with my friends as this new guy wanted to spend every possible minute with me. He became controlling to the point where I stopped all extra-curricular activities that I had so enjoyed. He also wasn't fond of the word "no" and pressured me into things I did not want to do. After a year and a half, I finally began to realize that this was an unhealthy relationship and I broke things off. Since I didn't really understand what he had done was wrong, I didn't talk about it to others. I became withdrawn and didn't know how to handle what had happened. A family crisis also occurred around this time, and that added to my already high stress levels. I felt as if control had been taken away from me and I found a way to cope with that. I started controlling everything in my life that I could, from my daily routine to every single thing I put in my body.

I started restricting the amount and type of food I ate. The less I ate, the more in control I felt. At times, I felt so vulnerable from everything that I had panic attacks and felt paralyzed with fear. I started exercising to quiet the thoughts in my head. My parents thought it was a rough time breaking up with my first boyfriend, and it was, but much more than they understood it to be. My older sister was the one who seemed to grasp that something was really wrong. She would make my favourite meals and take me out, encourage me to hang out with friends and have fun. If it weren't for her, I think things probably would have been a lot worse. My habits continued getting worse, but she was the life preserver that kept me from drowning.

My mom took me to our family doctor when I started complaining of chest pain, and he wanted to hospitalize me. I told my mom I wouldn't go and promised her I would get better on my own. Around this time, I met my future husband and we became high school sweethearts. He expressed serious concern about my eating and exercise habits and I felt the strength to try to get better for him.

I continued to struggle with my eating issues off and on until my mid-twenties. In university, I was getting sick of dealing with my issues through food and went to individual and group therapy. I slowly learned how to deal with things and not use food as a coping mechanism. My weight started fluctuating a lot, up and down, never really settling for long. I was never happy with the way I looked.

In 2005, I had a "wake up" call. I was diagnosed with thyroid cancer around the time I lost my father to a brain tumour. At first, all I could do was grieve my loss and feel sorry for myself. I went on a binging downward spiral, eating anything and everything. But after a year of this, I felt completely awful. So I made a change and started running. I would just run up and down the block once a week, then twice. I also started taking exercise classes at the local gym and noticed I was feeling a lot better. At the same time, I started to slowly change the way I was eating. Fewer frozen dinners, more fresh veggies. My husband and I started eating less junk. I started losing weight, but it was very slow and gradual, and something that just naturally occurred while I made these small but significant changes. After a year of this, I started to become very interested in food and how it works with our bodies. I had a few vegan friends that looked and felt amazing! I had been vegetarian off and on for several years, but could never give up my beloved cheese. Then I picked up T. Colin Campbell's book "The China Study." I promptly went vegan after reading it. I kid you not - the day I finished that book was the last non-vegan day I had. The extensive studies he did linking animal proteins to cancer growth and occurrence, especially to people who have already had cancer, was enough to make me swear off cheese for good. Going vegan was one of the best things I ever did. It opened up a whole new world to me. I went from being the pickiest eater ever to trying anything if it was vegan. I reached a healthy and stable weight, my hormones balanced, my allergies disappeared and I felt amazing.

I would love to tell you my story ends here... but it doesn't. I realized I loved nutrition and exercise so much that, in 2011, I quit my job to become a Group Fitness Instructor and a Registered Holistic Nutritionist. While I learned about nutrition, it triggered some old self-destructive feelings and I started restricting again without even noticing. I wanted to be "perfect" with my eating and became orthorexic. Friends (and even random people at the gym) started commenting about the weight I had lost.

As I was finishing my Holistic Nutrition Program, my husband was offered a job in California. I've never really dealt well with change since I was a teenager, as it makes me feel as if I have no control over a situation. And moving from Canada to California was a big change! Before we moved I was ecstatic, and my husband was beyond stressed at the prospect of moving to a new country and working for a new company. When we finally got here, he thrived and I withered. He had this exciting new job that he loved (and still does over 3 years later!) and I went from working two part-time jobs and going to school full-time to not being able to work at all with the immigration situation. I gradually started overindulging, otherwise known as "eating my feelings" and then over-exercising to compensate. I gained a lot of weight rather quickly and had a hard time dealing with it. I would restrict and binge and exercise and exercise and exercise. I suffered several injuries from exercising too much. I was always on edge and really depressed. My hormones were completely out of whack and I hadn't had my period in months.

It was on a trip to visit my family, just over a year after we had moved, that I finally realized I needed help. I decided to sleep over at my sister's house the night before I flew back to California, as her house was closer to the airport. It was also a lot closer to the gym and I wanted to get up really early to catch a boot camp class before flying home. That night, my mom called my sister's house to find out when she could see me again before I left. I told her I wanted to go to the gym before flying out, which meant I wouldn't see her my last morning. She had to be at work by the time I would get done my class at the gym. I could hear tears in her eyes when she realized I was picking the gym over her. I felt bad, but not bad enough to change my exercise plans. When I got back home, I realised how horrible it was to have done that, especially since she has a hard time with me living so far away.

With the encouragement from my amazingly supportive husband, I started treatment with an Eating Disorders Specialist in October of 2013. I was too ashamed to tell anyone else about it. I started seeing the doctor three times a week, with weekly visits to a dietician and therapist. It was really difficult at first, but I'm realizing now that I'm fortunate to have been given the option of out-patient treatment. At first, my doctor and I butted heads. She basically told me to stop being vegan as it would hinder my recovery. I was angry and didn't listen. But I thought a lot of things she said were a little ridiculous. I mean, two hours of intense exercise a day isn't so much, right? I had also almost cut out all carbs and wasn't having any snacks during the day (unless I was binging...). I was a complete mess. I was at high risk for osteopenia and at this point I hadn't had my period in well over a year.

In the past, I had tried to get better for others in my life; my sister, parents and husband. Ultimately, I realized the only way to have recovery stick was to want to get better for me. At some point during treatment, I did tell my sister and a couple of close friends that I was getting help. They were incredibly supportive and helpful, and always there for me, and I'm lucky to have them in my life.

Over the 16 months that I saw the Eating Disorders specialist, I started realizing my behaviour wasn't healthy for me. At first, I would lie to her, telling her I was gradually cutting down on exercise and eating more carbs, but I wasn't getting better. Very gradually, I started taking some of her recommendations and I started feeling better. It took a **long** time, but we finally started seeing eye to eye on things. One of the toughest things for me was to not have "no" foods. To not look at food as good or bad, but food/fuel for my body and to eat. When I see foods as "bad" it triggers me to try and avoid them at all costs until I finally break and binge on them. Sure there are foods that are more healthful than others, but I've learned that it's okay to enjoy a variety of things, and if I eat a little more of the foods that aren't quite as healthful, my body naturally starts to crave more healthful things. I'm still trying to figure out balance; it's definitely a work in progress.

I found that going to therapy was very beneficial in my healing process. It took a few tries, seeing a few different therapists, before I found one that I really clicked with. She helped me work through my issues and find myself again. Group therapy was also extremely helpful. I found nothing facilitated healing more than being surrounded by people going through a similar situation to my own. It made me feel less alone and helped give me perspective. Reading books eased me into a recovery mindset. "Unbearable Lightness: A Story of Loss and Gain" by Portia de Rossi really spoke to me. She bares all in this book and her unashamed and honest account of her recovery really helped me get past some of my destructive behaviours.

Ditching the scale was another part of my recovery that I think would help a lot of people who have any sort of body image issues. My doctor requested I give up the scale when we first met. I quickly realized that obsessively checking my weight was setting me up for failure. I would peek at the number between my fingers with a crushing feeling in my chest, hoping it hadn't gone up. If the number went up, it was time for a new round of restrictions and more exercising. If the number went down… well, much of the same. My weight was constantly yo-yoing up and down by 10+ pounds. I haven't looked at a scale in almost two years, my weight has stabilized, and I am more intuitive with my body by feeling how my clothes fit.

The thing I feel really helped with my depression, and ultimately my eating disorder, was getting a furry companion. I had nagged my husband for years for a dog. He wasn't crazy about the idea. When I started treatment, my Eating Disorders Specialist and my therapist both talked to me about getting a dog. My husband finally agreed, and it is the best thing I could have ever done for myself. My pup pulled me out of a very dark place and I will be forever grateful to her for this. Sunny loves me even when I'm wearing sweatpants and no makeup (that's a true friend), adores my off-key singing, follows me around when I clean to keep me company, and curls up on my lap when I read. She walks, hikes and runs with me and is pretty well with me all the time. She is my soul-dog.

When I started putting in an effort to take care of myself, my doctor eased up and we started getting along. I was finally told in January of 2015 that I graduated from treatment. I don't feel completely recovered by any means, but I feel pretty good about things, and will slowly continue on my recovery path. It's a lot of forward and backward, one step forward and two back at times; things go slowly, but I feel happier each and every day, and I am learning to love myself from the inside out.

* * *

*Kimmy is a holistic nutritionist looking to lead a healthy life and learning to love herself. She is passionate about helping people become healthier through fitness and food. Kimmy can be found walking the Northern California streets with her two best friends, Sunny & Terry (puppy and husband respectively). When Kimmy's not making and eating delicious vegan food, working on her blog, or volunteering, you may find her with her nose stuck in a good book. Please visit Kimmy at her website: www.rockmyvegansocks.com.*

# What Tough Times Reveal
## by Deborah Peniuk

When you look upon anyone, on any given day, do you decide based on their "cover" who they are? What have they gone through? Who were they at the start of this journey called life? I'm sure you've heard the saying - "Don't judge a book by its cover" and I am most certain you would never expect what lies on the pages beneath this cover of mine.

### Where to begin this tale?

Let's start at the beginning of learning about relationships and how suddenly sometimes they are just over.

Imagine you're twelve again. Life is reasonably good and the most complex thing is stumbling through puberty, keeping up with homework, and crushes.

Now imagine walking into the home you share with your parents and siblings, and everyone including your grandparents are sitting down around the kitchen table. Everyone looks grim and you get that icky feeling that something bad is about to happen. You want to turn away and perhaps try coming in again; maybe, just maybe that will change the outcome.

This is the point of big changes, when I stopped being a child inside and became on the fast track to being grown up.

My parents were getting a divorce. Life as we knew it was going to be forever changed. That moment defined how I thought for many years to come, and was probably the beginning of my feeling like I didn't deserve to be happy. I carried the heavy burden of thinking I was somehow to blame, not knowing that adult relationships are a whole different evolution of experiences, conversations, loving words, hurtful words, painful actions and sometimes foul deeds.

The human experience really doesn't prepare us well for that tidal wave. The next couple of years laid the groundwork and truly shaped the human being I was evolving into.

**Fast forward to high school graduation ...**

Nothing could have prepared me for meeting the man who would take my heart -- Martin, the first man I came to love outside of my family. The man I would give my virginity to and never have any regrets that he would be my first, my only, my forever. Little did I know what a huge gift I was giving to him, especially because I had held onto it until my 21st birthday.

Putting a pause on our facetime  and traveling thousands of miles away to Australia only made what was growing between us that much stronger. I was to be gone almost as long as we had been together, something that might have killed other new relationships, but not ours. Not even a snow flurry in 1992, that shut down most of the airports on the West Coast of both Canada and the US, could stop us from making snow angels once we got home, and hold onto each other for days after that.

The following year quickly evolved into the time we endured our first true hurdle as a couple -- my first deeply emotional loss as my grandmother passed away with cancer in the spring, images and emotions I can't ever erase from my being, and a recurring, crippling issue with hyperventilating. This would be the start of my true learning how to push through pain, focus on breathing and mental strength to move through the experience of loss. To this day I have moments when I shed tears, wishing that this woman, from whom I learnt my base of strength, was still here. As the moments of loss come and go, I hope she looks down on me as I try to do her proud.

Time passed as our relationship evolved and our love grew. It had its painful spurts, but trust was built, and we shared a bond and hope for a very rewarding future together. A lifestyle of heavier drinking and having a good time was slowly moving to times of coupledom, doing much healthier things, and sharing amongst friends with similar shared hobbies and activities.

Because we had built such a level of trust between us, and a friendship that went beyond our romantic ties, he felt that he could open up to me about something deeply buried, that was starting to surface. This is when I learnt about the various forms of abuse he had endured. Life was about to change in another direction as we moved through to a place of understanding, or at least we thought that is where it was taking us.

Whenever you hear of a child being sexually, emotionally, physically and mentally abused, what emotions surface? Mine could take me to places that would only land me in prison, were I to act on them. Imagine if you will, your most loved person opening up and sharing the life experiences that have also shaped who they are at that moment, and the shame and pain they must have endured just to survive. While I can never know truly the full experience to place blame, this has been something I could never wrap my head around. How does one take away the innocence of a child? What right does an adult have to molest a child?

In a very intimate moment, life was replaying some horrible memory for him, and a position of power enabled him to act out what I can only assume now was something he had endured. It is very hard to look at someone you love and see empty eyes looking through you, no longer at you, and taking some gratification that they were causing you pain. That act was being taken out on me, but I believe in my heart of hearts, because of our trust, that it had absolutely nothing to do with me but was an exorcism of some sorts for him, a way to communicate to me the depth of his pain.

I didn't know enough at the time that this was a sign we should have paid more attention to.

## Moving in together. No place to hide anything ... or was there?

The next year we decided to finally merge our homes together as we made more of a commitment to each other. Sadly, this would become another loss that we moved through together as his sister, who was seriously ill with Cystic Fibrosis and many secondary illnesses, took a huge turn for the worse the weekend we were moving our homes into one. Three residences to try and track us down, to rush us to the hospital to see her pass after a valiant battle for living. He was forever a bit broken from this experience, and a void started to grow the day she left us. I still miss the only "sister" I had loved for her courage and tenacity to show grace, creativity and love for her brother, the man we shared in our love for just a few years.

The next evolution for us was engagement and I was ready.

I can't ever complain that I don't know what an amazing proposal is like because Marty went all out. A beautiful dinner, tickets to see one of our favourite artists, Harry Connick Jr., an attempt to get up onstage to propose led to being turned away and coming back on bended knee at our floor seats mid-song to ask me to marry him. Of course I said yes, and after the concert finished he whisked me away to a bar where friends had been invited to celebrate our engagement with a dozen red roses, and champagne, of course. This led to a very late night, or early morning, phone call to both sets of our parents to let them know we were getting married. Everyone was happy...or so we thought.

## Loss of a Pregnancy

Completely unexpected but so very much wanted. I found myself pregnant early on in the year of our wedding, and while I wanted children I really wasn't sure if we were ready. I loved the idea that we had created something out of our love for each other, with all the other hardships we had come through. I wanted this for us and so it seemed, after the shock wore off, he did as well. But life seemed to have another plan for us. I miscarried at 3 months and it was something that forever changed me. But we took this and pushed forward because we knew we would try again after we had our wedding out of the way.

Jump forward to common law status, married in our hearts for almost 2 years.

Life had been moving forward as it should, and we were in the final stretches of reaching another milestone in our relationship. The last week before my 24th birthday was a whirlwind of happenings, including our double family wedding shower, full work schedules, another couple's wedding, last minute plannings, dress fittings, just trying to stay on top of it all.

I had gone out to a wedding dress fitting after a night of friends, family and lots of love. Our families had come together to have a wedding shower for us, and Martin had even given a beautiful speech to me and our families. I had met up with his mother to have a walk around our local lake, to talk of our plans over the coming weeks. I called home to let him know I was on my way back and got no answer. This wasn't unexpected as he was supposed to be sleeping before heading out to a graveyard shift for work.

I got home to an empty apartment. Something deep within me knew something was wrong. I raced around our apartment, calling out and looking in each room. I noticed his glasses, shoes and keys were gone but his wallet still sat on the dresser in our bedroom. Calls were made but no one knew where he was. A few hours later, a knock on the door revealed my building manager and a police officer. I felt my body start to turn to stone as I heard the words "May we come in? Unfortunately I regret to tell you that your fiancé is dead."

Breathe….5,4,3,2,1. This can't be happening. Why is this happening? I have to call his mother and father. Oh god…I can't tell my mom - this is the only other man she has ever allowed in her life since her divorce from my dad.

This was the most painful and defining time of my life.

Instead of a wedding, we had a memorial service that I hope gave some reflection of the amazing man that he was. I don't have all of my memories from that time as I know that some of them are still too painful to recall and my mind blocks them out. I spoke at his service and read the poem I had intended on reading at our wedding. I know that I did this because I have a recording of it but all I can recall is being aided up to the podium in the church. Those days became my autopilot days.

Ashes to ashes. I didn't get to have all of his ashes because I didn't have a small piece of paper that made my legal rights higher than his mother's. Unbeknownst to me, the funeral home had given his mother, by her request, ⅓ of his ashes. No urn; instead, I got a plastic bag with a zap strap , a sad representation of respect for me and for him.

I made my peace with so much of this time of my life because I had to. I had to move forward because I know that deep within there has to be more meaning to my life, but I am forever grateful for the love and the experiences I had with Martin. He showed me what love could look like in so many ways, and nothing I experienced will ever change that. Perhaps that sounds naive, but it's rather simplistic because I choose to not focus on all the pain and negativity. I now have a better understanding that there was a distinct sexual element to it all, stemming from the abuse from so many years gone by and a life with no guidance on how to deal with it, just a "sweep it under the carpet and forget about it" attitude by so many around him. Forget about it and move past. A confusion when stretched to be making the ultimate commitment of marriage and a life together, raising children.

I miss my best friend, my lover, my heart. He's gone and I'm still here.

The emotions - anger, pain, jealousy, rage- hurt so deep.

Suicide. The word alone can bring about tears, for some shame, and sadly for others pride. Just take a look at what is going on around the world today. This is something I will never understand.

I don't ever hide the fact that in the depths of my own person was despair after he left me. I thought my life as I knew it was over, and it was all just too much. Suicide wasn't a choice I had considered before in my life, and something deep in me would not let me complete the act. I couldn't leave so many behind just because I had experienced extreme loss. I was witness to the pain of those Martin had left behind, and knew that couldn't be my legacy as well.

This is an experience I wouldn't wish on my worst enemy. You will never have any clear answers because you aren't in that person's head to know what thoughts and emotions are pushing them to make the decision to end their personal pain, regardless of who it leaves behind.

Twenty years later I still have days of sadness creeping into my world, but I know that each experience has led me to be the person I am, and has given me the fortitude I seem to have developed along the way. I may have latent issues with crying and being "strong" but I know the power of release that tears have.

I've never found the same level of love and happiness again thus far, but I don't have the mindset that I never will; I just am much more appreciative of loving me. They say that showing love to yourself, not to be confused with being supremely selfish, will attract the right kind of person to you, who will show you the same level of love. I want to believe and trust in this. This has brought me to sharing the helpful bits of getting to a happier state of being that have worked for me, and that I have learned from so many others along this journey called life.

Deciding to take charge is the single most powerful, proactive thought you can have to get out of the loop of negative thinking.

Love never truly goes away, nor does the loss, but every day, if you choose to, it gets a little easier to bear.

Try to remember that your primary goal in life is to be happy. The only reason you have your desires, your wants, in the first place is that you think that having those things will make you happy.

Think about what makes you happy. Try to replace at least some of your negative thoughts with thoughts of things that bring you joy. There just might be plenty of those. It might be good to make a list of things you appreciate, the things you enjoy doing. And, if you are able to get to the point of making this list, your vibe will have naturally lifted quite a bit, and you may be able to take some inspired action to actually do one of those things that you enjoy.

Some tips to try and distract yourself from the negative thoughts/situations:

- Do something, anything, that takes your mind off of the supposed issue.
- Try taking a restful nap; soft nature sounds or earplugs and an eye mask work for me almost anywhere.
- Learn how to meditate.
- Watch a movie.
- Make your body move, get active and exercise. Go for a walk.
- If you have a hobby or hobbies, this is one of the best times to engage.
- Often doing something creative, like writing, painting, vision-boarding, or photography is the best antidote to pesky negative thoughts.
- Build a positive mental picture frame that you can access just like a memory card for your computer, full of happy times, images, sounds that bring you back to joy.

I'm always highly in favour of creative outlets, as they sometimes can give us a voice without words, that lends itself to purging and working through some of our most difficult challenges.

It sounds cliché, but I truly believe you can always take something good, something positive, out of a negative situation, so negative things too are a gift, but a gift cleverly in disguise. You can learn from everybody, especially from the ones that hurt you. You can use their negativity as fuel for your positive fire. You don't have to hold a grudge when somebody rejects you, regardless of the type of relationship. It's okay to be like "What a jerk for just dumping me like that and being totally careless about it!", but don't hold on to negative feelings for too long. Forgive. Do your best to try to understand where the other person is coming from, and realize that, more times than not, it's not about you at all.

Sometimes you simply have to go through difficult situations so that you can learn, come through the other side, and grow because of them. What do you choose to feel good or bad about? You, ultimately, are the storyteller of your life...always remember you have a choice, regardless of any situation.

* * *

*#OutsideTheBox Travel Maker specializing in Health & Wellness Retreats & Food & Wellness Escapes! Yoga+Wine+Food+Travel+Music=Happy Humans*

*Over the last 15 years, Deborah's travel consulting expertise and her leadership as an entrepreneur have been celebrated by various communities, such as Women's Post which is a magazine designed for professional women and The Karina Chronicles, who acquired her as one of their Brand Ambassadors. In addition to running AYA LIFE, Deborah writes articles and reviews for many Food and Travel events and products as well as a new lifestyle blog, Life, Bliss and All of This.*

# Becoming Sapphyre
## by Kayleigh Radatus

Once upon a time, there was a little girl. This little girl was different from most. She knew she was different, because she never really felt like she belonged, and because people always seemed to be looking at her strangely. She didn't know why she was different, or how she was different, only that she was.

As time went on, and the girl grew, she had many experiences that only amplified her differences, and the more different she became, the more she felt she didn't belong, and the more she was discouraged, excluded and hurt. It became a vicious cycle that would continue for years.

By the time the girl was thirteen, she knew enough, or thought she knew enough, to understand, to the very depths of her heart, that she had caused every hurtful event that had ever happened to her. This epiphany came on the day she received the phone call telling her that her Grandfather had died. All was suddenly clear. She had been too excited about visiting her Grandparents and other family. This was her punishment. She would carry the guilt over his death for decades.

Long before the death of her Grandfather, she had become skilled at suppressing who she was inside. It was enough that her life experiences had amplified her differences, so she did her best to hide her true self from the world around her. She was so good at it that most people had no idea of what she loved most in life. Her passion was music. She loved to listen, singing along, and losing herself in the power of all she heard and felt. Despite this passion, when the opportunity had come, when she was just nine years old, to audition to sing in a school play, she squashed the deep desire to do so, convincing herself that she could not sing and shouldn't even try. To do so would risk exposing who she really was, and that was far too dangerous. The reality of the situation was far worse, though. Her ability to hide herself from the world around her was slowly infiltrating her own awareness, concealing who she was even from herself.

As time moved on and all the memories of trauma and pain piled up with new wounds, she came to realize one simple truth; she was broken. Somehow, she existed as a cracked and broken person, damaged beyond repair, and had in fact been born this way. What other reason could there be, for all the awful ways she felt, and all the hard, painful experiences she'd had? It had to be the result of who she was. And yet, deep within, there burned a small spark, kept alive through small moments of light. That spark reminded her that there must be some part of her that was worthwhile, worth loving, worth staying alive for. She had people around her who said they loved her, and acted as if they liked her. They couldn't all be lying or just pretending to care out of some strange sense of obligation or responsibility, could they? Fortunately, the Universe seemed to support this idea that some part of her was worthwhile, for when the moments, minutes, hours or days came when she felt she just could not continue on, there was always someone there for her, whether she had reached out for them or not. One friend even became angry one day when the girl confessed her thoughts of suicide. The friend firmly stated; "If you do, I'll never speak to you again!", which prompted hysterical laughter on the girl's part; committing suicide would mean she was dead, so how could her friend speak to her? The moment became one of the many anchors that held her in place. Friends became her salvation, although many had no idea they were actually saving her life on a regular basis.

One day, she made a new friend. He was so open, warm and caring; and so nice to be around. He had this thing he would say whenever he was surprised or awed by something; "Holy Mackerel, Sapphire!", he would exclaim. The girl, who was now a young woman, had no idea where the saying came from, and was never sure if he was actually calling her "Sapphire" when he said it, or if it was just something he said. But slowly, ever so slowly, the name began to penetrate her subconsicous, and through the connection with her friend, she began to associate a certain strength and power with the name. Here was someone new who would feel no obligation to her, who liked her, and who (maybe) called her by this cool name.

Gradually, she pulled the threads of strength and power the name gave her together inside her mind, and fashioned them into a new persona: Sapphyre. Sapphyre was strong, confident, and powerful. In her own mind, this young woman, Sapphyre, was unique and amazing, while the girl who created her was not. Sapphyre was a young woman who could, and did, live the life she wanted to live, on her own terms. She changed the spelling of the name in her mind, and used it as an anchor, a shield and a cloak. Inside, Sapphyre became all the girl had ever wanted to be.

Yet she had no real idea how to be Sapphyre out in the real world. At night, alone in her bed, she would wrap herself in the cloak of being Sapphyre and dream of what it would be like to be her; to truly become her. The girl would dream the dreams of a future she didn't wholly believe could ever happen; yet living them in her own mind, wondering how they could exist, she found happiness within them.

In time, she began to understand how the persona of Sapphyre was something she could use to protect herself in difficult situations, how she could become so much more than she really was, when out in the world and wrapped in Sapphyre's cloak. So she did. She put on Sapphyre, wrapping this powerful vision around her weak and wounded self. Every time she did so, she grew a little inside. She began to see the amazing possibilities that life held and how, maybe, just maybe, there might be more out there for her. She no longer thought of how she might end herself, but instead, thought of how she might fix herself. There was still so much that was cracked and broken inside of her; so much that needed to be repaired and pulled together before she could ever begin to feel like she could be part of this world.

The task ahead felt like an insurmountable mountain peak, but that no longer mattered. By this point, she knew the information she needed to repair herself was out there, somewhere. She knew that if she searched, and learned, and worked hard, she could truly become Sapphyre.

I'm sure by now you've guessed that the girl in the story is me. My story is not so different from many others, because sometimes hard things happen in life. Dad drinks too much, your parents fight and split up. Return and split again, this time for good. All the while you're caught in the middle, not knowing how to take anything that is happening; so you block. You block the anger, and the sad, and the hurt that flows through you and swirls around you from everyone else. Accidents happen; outcomes are uncertain, and you, you have no idea of how to cope when both your parents are suddenly gone all the time, because you're just 3 years old. And because accidents do happen, your house burns down, and suddenly again; everything is gone. Yet again, you have no idea of how to cope because you're just 4 years old. So you block. You block the wound of being the little princess who can do no right, and you block the wounds of seeing your loved ones fight. You learn that there are people who like to hurt others, and you learn it isn't safe to trust. And because your life is just so damn full of experiences you just don't understand and don't know how to handle, you block it all. You block every damn thing until there is nothing there to remember but the smallest, tiniest, memories; snapshots in time that can only be safe. Protected moments that prove that both happiness and extreme hurt lived side by side. This is life for some, but children and teens who grow up that way don't know how to deal with it all, so frequently, they block. It can take decades to remove those blocks, and some never go away.

The experiences we have growing up shape the person we become. I want to be clear that I place no blame on anyone involved in any of the many and varied challenges I experienced growing up. It wasn't always that way. It took years of work and effort on my part to get to the place I am now. I love all of my parents, and count myself lucky to have all four of them and so many other amazing people in my life. I also need to say; I would not change anything about my life. I believe fully that I chose this life before being born into this time. I chose, just as we all do, the lessons I am learning.

I also believe that we choose some of the people who join us on our journey. I am extraordinarily blessed to have people in my life who have been there through some of the worst experiences of my life, and many of the best. I can't tell you how grateful I am for them, for that shared history that connects us, and for having people with me on this journey who truly understand "forever."

I have spent most of my life searching for answers, trying desperately to understand this world and my place in it. About ten years ago, I made a very important discovery; I was born with the highly sensitive personality trait. When I stumbled on Dr. Elaine Aron's book; *The Highly Sensitive Person: How to Thrive When the World Overwhelms You,* I'd never even heard of this trait. Dr. Elaine Aron, Ph. D. defines a "Highly Sensitive Person" (HSP) as someone who "has a sensitive nervous system, is aware of subtleties in his/her surroundings, and is more easily overwhelmed when in a highly stimulating environment." If you'd seen me in Chapters that day, you'd likely have given me another of those strange looks I used to receive all the time, because I was standing there, reading the first page of Dr. Aron's book, with tears streaming down my face. For the first time in my life, I understood that there was nothing inherently wrong with me, but that I am truly different from most people. I understood that day, that I am a product of my personality, my genetics, my environment and my experiences, and all of those elements combined make me unique, but not fundamentally flawed. I knew still, that I had work to do to fix the broken parts I had inside, but that was different from fixing who I was. The many life experiences I'd had growing up left me very damaged and in need of healing and repair. I also understand now, that those experiences likely would not have affected me as intensely or in the same ways, had I not been born with the highly sensitive personality trait. By the time I found Dr. Aron's book, I'd already done a lot of the work I needed to do to heal, but I wasn't finished yet, and maybe, never will be. But finding that book, and the information inside, was the key that finally allowed me to see myself as "normal but different" and in time allowed me to put my entire life into a different perspective.

The journey from when I first created the persona of Sapphyre until the day I found that book was a long and difficult one, and not one piece of it would have happened if I hadn't made one very important choice, and one equally important decision. I made a choice to change how my life would play out, and I made a decision to do whatever was necessary to create that change. I knew that if I didn't make some significant changes to the way I lived and behaved in my day to day life, I would never find true happiness. I would remain stuck in the world I currently lived in, and it contained more misery and pain than I could stand. I knew that in staying how I was, life would be one long, sad, lonely trek, and I wanted nothing to do with that vision of my future.

It's important to note that, at this point, I didn't actually believe I would find real, lasting happiness. I was so incredibly sad, depressed, angry and broken that I simply couldn't believe that the dreams others lived with every day, and believed in with all of their hearts, could possibly happen for me. One of the pivotable moments of change stands out in my memory as if it happened only yesterday, yet it occurred about twenty years ago. I was riding on the bus, stuck in sadness and hopelessness, and just wanting to get home. The bus approached my stop and as I began to rise to my feet, I glanced up and my eyes locked with those of a young man across the aisle. Then he smiled at me. I was stunned. Warmth bloomed in my chest where previously there was only pain. I got off the bus, watched it pull away and, feeling lighter inside, wondered at what had just happened to me. I don't remember if I even smiled back at that young man. I can only hope that if I didn't, he wasn't offended. He made such a difference for me with that one smile, and I hope he continues to smile at strangers today. Despite the constant emotional pain, sadness and hopelessness I lived with, somehow I knew there had to be a way for me to feel better than I did, and to live a life that was better than mine was. I would take any improvement I could get, believing that if I could just move away from all the awful feelings, that would be enough.

This is where being highly sensitive was a blessing in those years, even though I didn't know then that I had the trait. Highly sensitive people tend to have an intense awareness of the world around them.

They notice so many details about others that it is often overwhelming. But in this situation, I knew a better life was possible, even if I couldn't believe in it for myself yet, because I could see that life all around me. Most of the people I knew were not suffering like I was. They were happy. They were enjoying life and having fun despite the fact that they too had challenges in life. I desperately wanted some of that myself, and yet I was so deeply immersed in my own misery that I had no idea how on earth I'd ever find my way out to the life I barely dared hope for.

So, I followed the next logical step; I asked for information from others. I opened myself up to possibility and I asked for help. I was fortunate, at the time when I was beginning this search for information on how to transform my life, to have an extremely positive, upbeat person as my roommate. She was literally the most positive, happy person I knew. We were not just roommates; we were good friends, and one day I asked her how she maintained such a positive, optimistic attitude all the time. After all, she'd seen pain and hardship too, yet it didn't overwhelm her.

Unfortunately, she couldn't answer me. She told me she had no idea; being positive and happy was simply her way of being. This was, of course, a very frustrating answer for me, but soon after she came home with a set of personal development cassette tapes to listen to that would end up transforming my life.

The set was called "Self-Esteem and Peak Performance," by Jack Canfield. The day I began listening to those tapes was the day my world changed forever. Within these tapes was a whole new way of being, that I knew nothing about. The idea that I could actually change everything about how I perceived my world, interacted with it and even existed within it seemed too fantastic to believe. The whole concept was overwhelming and unbelievable to me, but I decided that I had nothing to lose by trying some of the tools Jack Canfield spoke about, starting with using affirmations. I was already at the bottom; there was nowhere to go but up.

I chose a special poem from a Hallmark wallet card my friend had given me as my affirmation. Usually, affirmations are positively worded statements that start with "I", but that was too far outside of my comfort zone for me to use. The poem was simply titled; "Believe", and it literally became my constant companion as I went about my day. I took the bus or walked everywhere back then; spending hours each day in travel, and that poem became the rhythm I moved to, everywhere I went. With every step I took, and every rumble and shake of the bus, the words of that poem tumbled over themselves in my mind, repeating over and over like the Hail Mary recitations of the devout Catholic with her rosary.

*Believe in yourself,*
*In the power you have,*
*To control your own life*
*day by day.*

*Believe in the strength*
*That you have deep inside*
*And your faith will help*
*Show you the way.*

*Believe in tomorrow*
*And what it will bring*
*Let a hopeful heart*
*Carry you through*

*For things will work out*
*If you trust and believe*
*There's no limit*
*To what you can do!*

With time, the poem's message of believing in yourself began to become part of me. I felt stronger, and more capable of creating the life I wanted. That summer, I made some significant, life-changing decisions, using the power that poem instilled in me. My life began to take on new meaning, and for the first time that I could remember, I felt true happiness, and actual hope for my future.

In this way, my journey of recovery, healing and empowerment began. Since that summer twenty years ago, I've spent countless hours studying personal development, and applying all I learned in order to continue the transformation. I now live a life I never imagined could have been possible, with wonderful family, including a beautiful daughter, amazing friends, work I love, a beautiful home, and many activities I love. This is not to say I don't still face challenges; I do. For me, life is a constant process of discovery and learning, and requires continual effort to maintain the mental space where I want to be.

Like many highly sensitive people, I tend to think deeply about life and all that goes on in it. It's part of my nature to reflect on existential questions, and it is easy for me to get caught up in negativity as a result. The personal empowerment tools I've learned over the years have been invaluable in dealing with this negativity.

Remembering that I always have the power to choose differently is key to maintaining my hold on happiness. Using affirmation tools helps keep my focus on how I want to feel, and what I want to create in life. Listening to my own intuition and taking constant and continual action keeps me moving forward, which also keeps me feeling positive. Lastly, remembering to look back every now and then helps me see all I've done, all I've created, and all that has changed. This remembering keeps my attention focused on all my life has become, keeping the existential depression I'm prone to at bay.

This is by no means a complete list of all I've learned and use in my daily life to keep me feeling good. To write a list like that would involve writing a whole book, but these tools are some of the best. They are the most powerful ones that I use consistently. Using them is like a daily cleansing and maintenance for the mind, heart and spirit. Just like we have to clean and maintain our bodies, our clothes and our homes, etc., we must do the same for the inner aspects of ourselves. These tools have the effect of sweeping away negative thoughts and emotions, releasing them instead of allowing them to stay stuck within me where they can build up to overwhelming levels.

We all have tremendous power within us to transform our lives. All we need is the awareness, and some ideas of what steps to take to create the changes we want. There are thousands of books written on the many steps we can take to create any change we desire, but any and all changes we create begin with three steps: the choice to change, the decision to begin doing something new, and taking action. Nothing else happens without these three steps, and it's possible that each step will have to be made repeatedly, as often as needed. I have had days where I've completed all three steps multiple times in one day, simply because I was so overwhelmed by my life as it was. This is okay. Every individual's journey is different, but it's important to remember that all else flows from these three elements. Without them, the only change that is created comes from outside of yourself when life happens to you, rather than you directing your life. I've lived both ways and, trust me, directing your own life is much better than letting life direct you. This doesn't mean you control every last thing, but you exercise your power to choose and take action to become happier. The Universe responds by helping you along; building you a life that is even better than you could have dreamed.

* * *

*Kayleigh is a Personal Empowerment Mentor, Certified Life Coach, and Certified Level 2 Reiki Practitioner. Her mission is to inspire hope and dreams, to encourage, support, and uplift, and to bring more joy, happiness and love into the world. In support of this mission, she created the "This Groovy Life" line of empowerment tools that includes; handmade semi-precious gemstone jewellery, pendulums and bookmarks, Remembrings Cards, and the Home Edition of her popular Beadiful Intentions Workshop. She also conducts one-on-one mentoring and Reiki sessions, empowering oracle card readings, and group workshops. She can be reached through her website; www.kayleighradatus.ca.*

# The Road Less Travelled
## by Laura May Roth

My life was bound to take me somewhere, but I didn't know it would take me this far. Finally, I'm here; it's morning in Thailand.

I wake up to the light crash of waves a few metres outside of our hut. If I manage to get myself out of bed, I'll catch the tail end of sunrise. I sneak away from beneath the covers, turning to look at Luke, who is still sleeping in the most glorious way that he does. I witness the sweat glistening off his freshly sun-kissed body. I'm so glad he is here with me.

I rustle through my over-packed bag and pull out a clean pair of cut-off jean shorts and a tee before heading out to our sand-covered porch. The heat is settling in for the day. It feels good to be here; to be away. I catch sight of the stray dog sleeping on our stairs and he somehow signifies a new life for me. I look out to the sea; it's the most beautiful view I've seen in a long time. The horizon is lined with palm trees along a cove with a little restaurant right on the beach. It's a perfectly hidden little oasis and I'm so glad we found it.

Sitting on the porch, looking at my new paradise, I take a deep breath of warm, salty air. It feels as pure as day compared to India. I stop for a moment to collect my thoughts. Everyone at home must be finishing work for the day or be busy running errands. I recall how awful I felt when I was back home as anxiety trickles through my system and my body tenses. I'm reminded of the ongoing 11-hour workdays, the responsibility of owning a house, of my dad being sick, and of the constant need to fit in. However, I recollect the comfort that came with routine and the satisfaction that came with each payday; but I still felt the looming need to change my life. I waited for each payday with angst.

Luke and I had been saving every penny since we met, in hopes that we would be able to travel for two years. I had dreamt of travelling the world since high school and, most of all, I wanted Luke beside me to experience it with. At night, we would sleep under a map of the world and dream about our trip. We would talk about all the things we would do with our free days, about how we would sail, learn to scuba dive, read books, and meet other travellers. We were love drunk; we'd sip expensive wine, getting carried away by trying to pronounce the places we'd visit. We would count our money and map out our journey together. It's the first time I could recall feeling loved.

Looking back, I remember how good it felt good to quit work, sell my house, and get on that plane. My gaze returns to the beach as I feel the sand between my toes and clamor into the nearby hammock tied between two trees. I'm serenaded with a view of calm emerald blue water that wraps along the bay as I let go of my thoughts and watch fishermen come in with their catch for the day. I start to meditate using the techniques I had learned in the previous months about breathing and letting your thoughts wander, accepting feelings that come as they arise and letting them release. I witness the golden amber tones of the sand that glisten in the sun. This is the road less travelled; this is where I want to be.

With the sun warming my body, I feel the hurt that has been locked up inside of me fade with each new breath. I realize I've been holding onto the pain of losing my mother as a child and trying to cope with my father's illness. Everything that once hurt me was still somehow living inside of me. I take a long, meditative breath and feel a steady calm fall over my body. Suddenly my mind takes me back to India: the chaos, cows that lined the road, trains, and defiant monkeys. My preconscious mind starts to relive the experiences I had.

For a month Luke and I had been travelling around India, hopping on buses, hitching rides, and constantly surrounded by foreign, unique, and beautiful things. Still in the early stages of travelling, everything was novel and exciting to us. I recall the day we boarded the Kalka–Shimla Railway that brought us to north-west India. The train crept along a steep vortex of mountains that cusped the Himalayas while we ate warm curry. The ride was exhilarating.

Moving from trains to buses, each leg of our journey was met with the three Vs: views, vertigo, and vomiting. For me, whizzing around corners at warp speed on transit was far from easy, and often left me hanging out the window, trying to hold on to my warm curry. The farther we travelled, deep into the north-west mountains, the fewer rail guards and intersections there were, and the more I hung out that window. Although it was the road conditions and driving that was making me sick, I felt as though my body was purging itself. The stress that once existed in me, the grief I still hung onto, the sadness I felt; it was all coming out. I felt my body surrender as it purified itself.

When I close my eyes, I can picture myself back on that lime-green weathered bus that gripped the side of the road. I was scared; it seemed that—at any moment—we would surely tip over into the deep valley. In that fear, however, I found acceptance; the realization that I had no control over what would happen to our bus or how the driver would navigate the roads. The bus creaked with each turn, the seats were lined with rusty springs that threw us like rag dolls from one side of the bus to the other. In grander view, our journey represented the fear I had of losing my father. I had no control over the outcome; the fate of that bus or that of my father.

Passing Nepal we headed farther north to the edges of Tibet. Each new village marked a milestone in our journey and represented an obstacle that I had overcome in order to be there. Looking up, there were many more roads ahead, and just as many villages. With my head out the window, I wondered how much longer our ride could be. It echoed my eager need to leave home. I longed to be somewhere else and be someone else, someone who no longer had the pain I did. It had been hours like this and I was blistered with exhaustion. I clutched the window frame and vomited for the seventh time as the locals watched me in pain. I had hardly learned any Pahari phrases while on the trip but looked over to the locals and flashed them a smile to indicate I was okay.

It seemed our lack of linguistic capability would also soon start to show. As our journey continued on, I tried to communicate with the bus driver that a rest stop was welcomed and much needed. Despite my attempt to state the obvious, he continued to twist and turn his head with each word I spoke. Carrying on, I would point outward to the road, and then back to myself in an attempt to gesture that I needed to go to the bathroom. I was desperate. It seemed that, at any moment, we would pull over, but those fleeting moments turned to hours. With each bump of the road, I tried not to wet my pants. I was trying to think of a solution.

Luke and I were stationed at the back of the bus and had brought with us a small waterproof bag that kept our camera, passports, and electronics dry. I quickly started to remove the stuff from our bag as I explained to him that it was my only chance.

Luke reluctantly agreed to my plan.

Trying to keep as concealed as possible, I shimmied my pants down, ensuring no one noticed me. We were travelling in a conservative area and if caught doing what I was about to do, it would cause problems I could not afford. I looked up to see the bus driver peek at us through his rearview mirror. Despite the fact that the winding narrow road needed his undivided attention, he continued to look back at us. With Luke holding the bag beneath me, I stood up slightly and had the most enjoyable pee of my life. I looked down at Luke's face annoyed and embarrassed. Once I finished, Luke signaled that he was ready to throw the liquid out the window. I kept a sharp eye on the bus driver darting his gaze from the road back to us. The moment he looked away I gestured to Luke to throw my urine out the open window. Not wasting a second, he lifted the bag to the window and out it went. We turned our heads in enough time to notice a man less than 3 metres away on motorbike, now covered in urine. Luke and I were in utter shock but immediately broke out into an unstoppable laughter. I felt horrible, but Luke and I agreed that this would be a story for the books. Later on that ride I thought of the irony of the situation. The notion that one person's pleasure could be another person's pain suddenly took on a new meaning for me.

Without any further incidents, we finally reached Sarahan, a small picturesque village in Himachal Pradesh perched at the top of the Himalayas. It was late and there was no electricity. I couldn't see anyone or anything, and my toes tingled in pain from the cold. The bus driver kindly directed Luke and I to a local temple a few blocks away where we could arrange a stay in exchange for a small donation.

Arriving at the temple, a man greeted us and started to give us a tour. We were exhausted and I needed to wash my clothes. We were hungry and wanted a hot shower. But, the reality was that I needed everything I was wearing to keep the heat in, that there was no food, and that I certainly would not be showering. During that ominous night at the Bhimakali Temple, Luke and I worked by candlelight, carefully etching out the travel route we would take back to New Delhi and across Asia. It was one of our last nights in India and we would soon spend the year in South-East Asia before moving to Australia for another year. Although it was a travel journey that I once yearned for, I was also on a path of self-love and healing.

Waking up the next morning on top of the salutary mountains I felt I had reached a spiritual place where I met myself for the first time. I was finally ready to let go of the weight and worries that had been locked inside of me for years. That day I sat down and wrote my father a letter. I wrote him until my pen ran out of ink. I didn't stop once.

Taking a concluding breath, I step out of my meditative state. The peaceful sounds and colours of the Thai beach greet me and I hear Luke calling me for breakfast.

Later that day Luke and I learned that my father had passed away. I realized, like on the bus, I had no control over his fate.

I ran back to our hut and rifled through my bag desperately searching for the letter I had written to him. I never sent it. I found it at the bottom my pack and pulled it out and held it close to me. I cried, knowing that everything I wanted to say to him was scribbled onto those pages. They were the last words I had for him.

I look up to the sky and felt he was somehow with me in that moment. I felt he would be there for me always, watching me travel and looking down on me each step of my journey.

* * *

*Laura May is a Guelph native with a knack for adventure. In 2013, Laura May completed here Masters in International Affairs from the University of Ottawa. She currently works for the Federal government in the nation's capital pursuing her career in the area of foreign policy. Born with an extra travel chromosome, Laura May has ventured to over 50 countries. She's sipped wine in rural Italy, backpacked through the Middle East, and dove with sharks in the Galapagos. She even celebrated Christmas on the Trans-Siberian Express. Taking pictures and revisiting old travel journals inspired Laura May's "The Road Less Travelled."*

# White Towels
## by Valerie Senyk

I don't know that I can live with this guilt anymore…

No, it's more than that. What I'm feeling is deeper than guilt; it's a question of how is it that I am here, toweling my hair after a hot shower in my white bathroom, while other women elsewhere in the world haven't even got clean water to drink. But it's more than that, too – and this is so easy to misunderstand - because beyond guilt it is pain, and it is weight, and I don't think I can bear to live my life as it is, in the world the way *it* is: the pain of the world, the groaning for God's sake of the world …

This moment reminds me of my coat story of twenty years ago. I've always put this glow around it in my memory, like it's some insight into the nature of my soul: my goodness, my generosity – or some such garbage. But thinking about it now makes me ashamed because it's so feeble. It goes like this: when I was young I splurged in a way that wasn't my habit and purchased a stylish new coat I had seen in the window of a store. But when I wore it I began to feel this unbearable weight, because I would pass people on the street who looked poor and shabby…and I realized that there were those in the world who could never hope to have such a beautiful coat as mine. I felt like a traitor walking about with this piece of vanity on my body. So when it accidentally ripped under the arm while holding a strap above me in a crowded bus, I was grateful. I could return it to the store, say "No thanks, look, it's obviously flawed," and go back to wearing my grandmother's old coat, which made me look like a WWII refugee. But at least I had no guilt.

This is the kind of garbage that resides in my head, a result of being brought up in our innocuous culture, where really everything is peachy keen; where my grandparents came – and I can't forget this – for the sake of their children and their children's children, away from the oppressive and hunger-stricken lives they were living. So maybe my guilt is really their guilt – ah, lovely Western rationalizing – and I've simply inherited my grandparents' guilt over leaving a homeland behind them in order to come to Disney World!

But, no, it wasn't Disney World for them living in a tiny, creaky house in inner city Winnipeg by the river, and later by an overpass for God's sake, and Baba bearing six children and going out to clean houses for the rich who despised her Slavic tongue, and later, even when she was quite old, to clean floors and toilets at the hospital. All this despite losing two children – William and Mary, who are in the same photograph as my mother as a baby; despite the cancer and diabetes that took hold of her body sometime in the process. She still managed to bake Easter bread, kneading the thick dough with her small hands, preparing feasts for the entire family... But how did she *feel*? Did she despair? Or my grandfather with his bad back and cane; did he despair when the overpass was built right outside their front door, and fumes from cars and trucks permeated the neighbourhood?

But that's long ago; that's another story, yet I don't know if it's part of my story, or if my story is part of the world's story, and if so, is it an irrelevant and sickly part of the story?

What sacrifices, what acts of heroism have come from me? And I dare to say I suffer because maybe I'm suddenly having trouble finding *meaning* in my work, the work I once loved, and sometimes I don't even care what I do because it's all part of, it's all feeding into Disneyland anyway.

Because outside this bathroom is a reality that I can only tentatively try to know, a reality that is the exact polar opposite of the side of the globe we're on, and there are no white bathrooms and women carefully toweling their hair, there are no drugs in a medicine cabinet to take care of every twinge in the body and twitch of the nerves, no costly lotions to rub into the skin as part of a bedtime regime adopted by countless women on this side of the globe who fantasize they have no age lines, sagging necks, large backsides or lack true beauty - - I know, I know, this is very judgemental!

I was with my friends Pam, Julie and Angel a few evenings ago. We were having a nice chat about ourselves, our kids, and suddenly, in a lull, I actually blurted out that I could hardly bear living in the world any more...Then I realized that that probably sounded a touch neurotic, and I tried to backtrack, make light of it – but I know I couldn't erase the thread of despair in my voice, I couldn't undo *that*, even though normally I am so careful about what my voice gives away. They found it difficult to respond; I could see that. I too would have trouble knowing what to say. I changed the subject.

A similar impulse happened at a meeting at work. We were discussing a new proposal, and it was all very animated and positive, and I felt, 'okay, now my colleagues and I are having a really good exchange here, so maybe I can just introduce something a little more intimate, like: is anyone else here feeling the weight of the world, anyone else getting these dizzy, ready-to-die feelings about it?' But as soon as I thought that, I knew that everything good that was going on would stop, just stop...and they'd all stare, and wonder if I was joking, or if the flakiness they suspected in me from the first was finally revealing itself in a full-blown meltdown.

Unfortunately, our world is full of these moments in which you feel trust, friendship, love – but if you were to say something really true and difficult for the hearer, that would all change.

Our son remarked today while he and I played cards that he liked me with a bit of attitude. Hah. This attitude is the visible result of my invisible conflict. It has to go somewhere... I was talking on the phone to my artist friend earlier in the day – Crystal, who's living in Toronto. I was missing her, and her luminous spirit and Mennonite values. I was trying to describe the inner thing that's happening to me, and I got this visual image of a drip of molasses winding itself, sticking itself, along a thin glass cylinder. As though this is a picture of me right now. When I saw the image in my mind it was just a twisting shape. I didn't know it was molasses. But the colour is right. And now that I think of it, maybe talking to *Crystal* inspired this subconscious glass cylinder that my molasses-angst was wrapping.

Truly I'm sick of myself. Yesterday I was looking for a collection of beads I'd purchased three, four years ago. I went through unpacked boxes in the basement, and inadvertently I found my whole life in them. There are countless journals, letters, photos, mementoes – my whole life. But as I sifted through this record I became embarrassed. I thought, if I were to die tomorrow, my husband and sons would sooner or later have to deal with the detritus of my life, and then they'd all know just how small and petty I am. When I really think hard about it, it's likely I have never felt or done a truly selfless thing in my entire life.

In memory, our Baba was undemanding, and focused her activities on everyone else. Her soft bulk moved throughout her extended household with delicacy and kindness. She fed and watered all who came to her door. Two of her children had died in their youth; the four left had complicated spouses and families. There was always a sense of crowding; too many adults and their children needed her protection or common sense. She gave with both hands. When she became ill, no one knew about it, until near the very end. She continued to work and cook and clean, and never complained. I was eleven when she died. I did not converse with her, because I could not speak in her tongue. She spoke little, anyway. She only intercepted if arguments broke out. The kitchen was her domain. My mom wept hard at her passing.

If I start feeling rotten, getting sick, my functioning level lowers drastically and I get scared. I panic, just a small panic – the kind that doesn't stop me from doing what's necessary, but that engenders a sick at heart feeling. From the smallest thing, I irrationally fear my world crashing down into some nightmare situation. And why? I have so much. Maybe it's too much for me to handle. Maybe it's like the new coat – I can't live with this wealth until the world gets fixed.

Yet I'm not a guilty person by nature. When people close to me have erred – really gone off the rails – I've tried to dissuade them from any guilt. I am determined that God, or that Largeness-Out-There, is Merciful and will forgive the most grievous of sins…But there are sins of commission, and sins of omission, and I feel within myself a vacuum of non-doing that shrieks louder than my old cigarette habit, my wasteful, vain purchases, my toilet flushes…

Before dinner tonight I was washing a vegetable under the kitchen tap: a zucchini. I was scrubbing it with a cloth, because of our boy's allergic reactions to the pesticides on all our produce. I wanted it to be pesticide free. And then I saw all the water running into the drain, all the cold, fresh clean water that I was using up to wash one zucchini. And I had a sudden image of millions of drains across the continent with tons of water being washed away, wasted, in our over- developed world. It was terrifying. I placed the zucchini carefully on the countertop. I didn't know if I had scraped away enough of the pesticides, but I could not bring myself to use any more water.

There's a photo I clipped from the front page of the newspaper of a little boy, maybe four or five years old, being held in an adult's arms, somewhere in Afghanistan. His head is shaved, and one eye is squinting as he looks toward the camera. He reminded me of my first grandson…

I can't explain the empathy I felt for this unknown child. I knew nothing of his plight, nothing except certain sanitized media reports of what was happening around him. But I yearned for – what? The photo to come alive, giving me the power to reach out my arms to enfold him, to save him?

With what: my white towels?

I have imagined myself there, in Afghanistan. I am among many dark skinned, veiled women and boisterous children. I am there to be of service. I'm smiling with them, listening to their stories…And sometimes we speak about the need for justice, not just here, but for the whole world. I am *with* them, it's where I belong, it's where I'm needed, and I feel that I would die with them, if necessary. I want to sacrifice what I can.

…and get rid of the weight in my soul.

But – but – it is unlikely I will ever go to Afghanistan.

So…okay…I'm doing my bit, and I have to be satisfied with that. I do not RUN the water, I do not flush every time, I'm composting and growing vegetables in the summer, I'm recycling – clothing, furniture, objects – anything I can. It doesn't feel like much…I'm still aware of the thick particulate matter in cities like Beijing and Shanghai and Dubai; I'm aware of Syrians crowding into camps to escape the war with minimal shelter; I'm aware of the melting of icebergs and the plight of polar bears caught on ice floes – YES, I'm aware! But I cannot stop these things – they're too large – too far – too much for one person.

But here I am, with you, and you, and you, and if each of us does our little bit, our conscious part, I have to accept that, I HAVE to!

\* \* \*

*Valerie earned a BFA in Fine Arts while a single parent, and an MA in Drama from the University of Saskatchewan, and taught Theatre at universities in both Saskatchewan and Ontario for over 20 years. She is an actor, director, performance poet, and visual artist. She's been published in many journals and has a collection of poetry,\* I Want a Poem\*, published by Vocamus Press, 2014. She is blessed with three amazing sons and six grandkids, and attributes her continued learning and creative adventures to her long-standing adherence to the Baha'i Faith.*

# The Lighter Side of Darkness:
## My Journey to Wholeness
### by Jessica Sgrignoli

Ah, where to begin? It's never been easy for me to spill the beans about my own insecurities and shortcomings. I have never been one to let myself be vulnerable, ask for help when I need it, or dare admit I don't have *all* the answers.

Some might say I have lived a pretty privileged life. I was raised by the most hard-working, tough loving mother I could imagine; a mother who would've done anything for her two girls, putting her kids first, above all else. I had food on the table and a roof over my head; a privilege in this part of the world, which I know I took for granted growing up. I grew up making friends quite easily, making sure to befriend everybody.

So what makes my story worthy of being heard? I firmly believe that everyone has a story, and if you don't think you have a story to tell, you probably do. One thing is for sure— no person (myself included) is exempt from the human experience, regardless of privilege. At one time or another, I am pretty sure that everyone one of us has had a very real, visceral experience of disappointment, unworthiness, insecurity, emotional turbulence and stress. And as a first-hand observer of all of these, I qualify myself as a worthy candidate.

Growing up without a father from the age of 7, I felt a sense of lack, poverty, as though I were missing something that I *knew* all others kids who grew up with fathers had. While I wasn't quite sure what this missing piece was, I was pretty sure I didn't have it, and I was determined as all hell to figure out what it was.

This may come as a surprise for some, but seeking approval from others has been the bain of my existence for the past 15 years. I'm determined to shed this heavy layer once and for all. I have nothing to hide because, actually, some of my most intimate moments and meaningful lessons learned have come when I let my guard down. If you stand completely raw and naked in front of another, this gives an unspoken permission for them to do the same. As Alisa Starkweather, a leader of women's empowerment, puts it, "Vulnerability and transparency is our strength— not hiding or covering up. It's a messy place to be who we really are…it's difficult to expose oneself— but it's worth it. Because it's our humanity. And this means every single part of our humanity— not just the parts we think other people are going to admire…" If at least one person hears my story and can relate, I consider my mission complete.

As you read through the pages of my mind, please know that I intend not to offend, if the subject matter relates directly or indirectly to you. My only intention is to speak the truth; to be true to myself. I wish not to censor or sugar coat my thoughts and feelings because I have done this for too long. It is nothing personal. Every person who has come into my life has served a valuable purpose, and I wouldn't change a thing about anyone or any decision I have made.

I guess the easiest place to start would be back at the beginning. The very first visceral experience of emotion that I recall left a mark on my heart that I'll never forget. When I was 2 years old, my father was diagnosed with Schizophrenia (although the way I see his 'dis-ease' and how society views and labels it are two totally different stories). When I was 7, he was asked to leave our family. At the time my mother was doing what she felt best. Deep down inside I don't think he wanted to leave, but he wasn't making any real effort to stay, either. My father's half-absent, confused presence and refusal to take his medication had started to take its toll on my mother.

I'm not so sure my sister and I really knew what was going on until he was gone. I remember that day like it was yesterday. I was so angry and upset at my mom for kicking him out that I crawled under my bed, wailing at the top of my lungs. All I wanted was for someone to acknowledge my pain and sorrow, to hold me, or at the very least, tell me everything was going to be okay—anything! But much to my disappointment—nothing. After what seemed like hours of wailing in desperation, without so much as a walk-by from anyone, I finally threw in the towel; I was exhausted and ready for bed. That night I slept like a baby. I never cried like that again.

When I reflect back on those early years and throughout high school, I realized that I not only missed my dad, but was embarrassed and afraid of him. After he was asked to leave, he would show up at late hours of the night and anxiously ring the side doorbell, waking us up in the middle of the night. Even to this day, whenever I hear that doorbell ring, I still jump. It brings me back to those nights I would wake up to the feeling of shock and fear running through my body. Why would my Dad do such a thing? Doesn't he have any sense in him not to do this? When my mom would answer the door on his unexpected visits, he was usually incoherent and somewhat aggressive. He wanted to see us, but my mom refused. She was fearful and anxious about him, and so I followed suit and took this on, too. Who was this man, now? We had so much fun together when I was young, he was my best friend. But now a complete stranger, and one who was actually starting to scare me. A father is someone who is supposed to protect you, but instead I felt the opposite. I found myself in a constant state of anxiety and fear about seeing him, not to mention running into him in public when I was out with my friends.

During my adolescent years of high school and university, I never did feel quite good enough. Insecure, inadequate and unsure of myself, I desperately sought approval from others to feel good about myself and rarely spoke up about what I wanted for fear of being disliked. I would bend over backwards for just about anyone — a true doormat, especially when it came to pleasing romantic partners. When someone would ask me to jump, I'd say "How high?" I sometimes felt as though I was missing a protective encasing that I believed all other girls received from their fathers growing up. I carried around this pervasive feeling of fear and nervousness; a strong sense of uneasiness about being in my own skin that I just couldn't put my finger on. These insecurities played over and over in my head like a broken record. Stop already! At the end of the day, I wound up feeling so exhausted, trying to please everyone but myself. I felt exactly the way Dr. Tom from *Being Erica*, describes it in episode five of season one. "It's like you are in a boat, you've got this one ore over here, and it's just rowing and rowing and rowing, furiously fuelled by everyone else's expectations. And that's never going to stop but it's kind of got you going around in circles, but if you want to move forward you also have to row with the ore that represents how you see yourself."

My mother did her best to play the role of both mother and father; I think she did a damn good job with the resources she had. She hid her disappointments well, in order to be strong for my sister and me. I don't remember ever seeing her cry. Seeing tears at home was foreign to me. Based on my early experiences, I didn't know what a healthy outlet for sadness looked like. Instead, I just held it in. I felt stuck. I learned how to be strong and independent in the face of sadness and adversity, in order to protect myself. Even though I had a gentle nature on the inside, I formed a hard shell around me in order to make it in the world. I distanced myself from my own emotional states in order to get on with it, and refused to express my emotions because I didn't think there was such a thing. I was really good at never letting anyone in close enough to see the real me.

Not being able to healthily express my emotions meant I could fly off the handle at any moment, without warning. I'll never forget my first raging episode as a child. I don't think anyone who was in the house that day will ever forget. Hell, I don't even think the neighbours will forget. I remember being sent to my room for something I did wrong, most likely swearing or telling my mom where to go. I'm not proud of it. I had a fire inside me that was about to erupt! Underlying, I was still angry about not having my father. The first thing I thought of was to slam something as hard as I could, and my closet doors bore the brunt of it that day. Oh, if those closet doors could talk! I felt my rage dissipating as I had an outlet for my anger, my emotions. Man, was that ever satisfying. But wait, not so fast there, Jess. This act of slamming doors was not okay as far as my mother was concerned. My mother must have been wondering, in total disbelief, who is this child of mine?

I was left in my room to cool down until it passed, and was later disciplined for acting out in this way. This dramatic episode imprinted in me that it's not okay to express anger. And so, I held it in as best I could, for fear of being punished; un-loved.

I continued to stuff my feelings of anger and sadness all throughout high school and university; I dared not show this side of me to anyone. I would literally stuff down my emotions with food because I didn't know how to deal with them. I would notice the feelings rise up from my guts, as it made its way to the throat to be expelled—and nothing! No words, no expression— nothing. I came up flat. Uhh! How frustrating. Feeling frustrated, yet numb to act, I would stuff myself silly with food because I wanted to express myself, but despised not being able to. I had to get rid of this contradiction immediately. Yes. I had bypassed the turbulent, uncomfortable emotions one more time. At times I felt two-faced, hiding from others to scarf down my favourite comfort foods— cheese, cheese, and more bricks of cheese. There is nothing quite as satisfying as a nice brick of cheese to drown your sorrows. I worried if anyone would catch on. What was I trying to forget, not to feel?

It wasn't until second year university that the constant competition between classmates, uncertainty about the future and my personal striving for perfection started to really take its toll. I began to have what I know now as panic attacks. I was working too hard, stressing too much and taking life way too seriously. Nothing was ever good enough. This uncanny feeling of being engulfed into a deep, dark, black hole would be enough to make anyone go mad. A feeling of drowning; I was caught in a nightmare I couldn't escape from and the walls were caving in on me. And most frustrating of all, I wanted to know why everyone else had it all figured out. Or, so I thought.

What came next was a saving grace I'll never forget. In third year I decided to take up Eastern Psychology, and the events that followed changed my life! Coming home after the first day of lecture on meditation, I was totally blown away. Being introduced to a completely new way of seeing the world, I felt like I had gotten a brain transplant.

For real! My healing had officially begun and there was no turning back, and why would I? From here I went on to become a Yoga Teacher. I began exploring different styles of Yoga, meditation, attending experiential workshops on Ecopsychology and Non-violent Communications. What I uncovered from taking the time to delve deeply, with the right tools, into the parts of myself that I had cast away, astonished me. I discovered alternative therapies such as Family Constellations and Women's Groups, namely, the Guelph *Full Moon Women's Circle* and *Women Within*, which were healing beyond words. I was meeting fascinating new people everywhere I turned. I was beaming with gratitude for my new-found path. Through Family Constellations, I discovered that hiding or being embarrassed of my dad was like hiding from myself; rejecting half of myself to the darkest corners where it couldn't be seen, along with the good parts.

When I embarked on this journey to look for what was wrong with me, as if almost bracing myself for it, I uncovered what was right with me. Ha! Imagine that. What I gained through delving into the shadows of insecurity, guilt, grief, anger, self-criticism-I gained tenfold in strength, brilliant resilience, and a positive outlook with an unbreakable spirit. You really can make rich compost from the crappy situations, if you are willing to make your way in there. And digging through the dark places really does gave way to the light on the other side. This reminds me of another quote I recently read, by Pat Schneider, "The holy work is going into the dark… learning how to be for ourselves what others cannot be for us." Each one of us is whole and complete just the way we are, and if we learn to love ourselves unconditionally, first and foremost, the rest will fall into place.

Had it not been for me searching out the missing pieces, I would have never come full circle to see the relationship with my mother who had been right there in front of me the whole time. I realized that what I had been yearning for all these years was being able to ask my mom for a hug when I really needed it. To be able to cry in my mother's arms without feeling awkward (seems so simple, right?).

I also came to discover that when I allow myself to be vulnerable, and let the feelings come, they suddenly disperse and create new space for change and expression to flow in unexpected, extraordinary ways. Being vulnerable *IS* courageous and it has the ability to transform us. So, the next time you feel yourself running away from your feelings wherever they are in your body, stay put, with all the courage you can muster, and just allow yourself to feel it. This is your body's higher intelligence, a way of communicating with you. Even if the pain feels like too much to bear, if you stay present with it for as long as you can, it has the ability to transmute and crack towards the light. If not today, there is always another opportunity to try again tomorrow. Life is a journey and we keep on learning the lessons until our life is complete. At one point I believed that since I had done the work of going into the dark shadows and uncovering the messy bits, I was set for the rest of time. Not long after was I quickly corrected.

So, what might you say was the greatest lesson I learned from journeying into my darkest fears, the great unknown? There will be moments of triumphs and ecstasy, and times of loss and suffering. It is not what happens to us in our life but how we choose to perceive the situation and, therefore, react to it. Sure, there are days when I avoid my Yoga mat like the plague and fall back into unhealthy habit patterns. But each time presents an opportunity to see the situation more clearly than the last. Fear is a natural reaction to moving closer to the truth, but if I allow myself to remain present to my immediate experience, I uncover priceless virtues I least expect, on the other side.

\* \* \*

*Jessica graduated from Brock University with a Bachelor of Arts major in Psychology. She is currently enrolled at the Canadian College for Massage and Hydrotherapy, and wishes to incorporate Massage Therapy into her current practice in the field of Alternative Medicine. Her desire is to support female helping professionals on their healing journey to wholeness through the use of Yoga therapy and Ayurvedic body treatments. Jessica believes self awareness and unconditional self-care to be key components to restoring physical, mental, emotional and spiritual equilibrium. Please visit Jessica at www.journeytowholeness.ca.*

# Learning to Love
## by Evelyn Taylor

Life is a series of struggles, and my healing has been ongoing and cyclical. From the first scrapes and bumps to heartbreaks to deaths, to change. I, like you, have been through many struggles. Deaths of friends and relatives, near death of myself, rape, molestation, divorce, isolation and bullying have all come into my life and left their marks. Some I have handled well, some not so well; others I brought on myself, or at least felt I did. All of them have shaped me.

When I look back at the struggles I've endured, I notice that the most challenging ones for me have been those that involve relationships and, like any other reasonable human being, I largely blame my parents.

Don't get me wrong, I love my mom and, despite all of the insanity and pain, I somehow still love my dad, but they definitely messed me up. They gave me all that they could, and I am grateful for what they did give me, but I still have difficulty accepting that there was a lot they couldn't give.

They couldn't give me a functional model of love and, at some times, they couldn't give me love. They could not illustrate how to have friendships and a partner at the same time. Their challenges became my challenges. There were different details, and at different times, but at the core, they were similar struggles. Both of my parents struggle with self-love.

My mother was anxious. She had lived as an English person in a separatist neighbourhood in Quebec, with parents who constantly devalued anything deemed impractical. An only child, she was often treated as a possession, and sorely lacked warmth and love. Her anxiety was palpable and, though she tried to cover it with smiles and good intentions, it lingered, unresolved.

My father was adopted into a chaotic and troubled family. Abused on many levels, his anger was never far away. Though he was a dreamer and wonderfully whimsical at times, he often gave in to abuse and recklessness. When he was happy, everything around him was magical but as soon as he wasn't, his presence inspired fear and darkness beyond anything else I have experienced.

I often wondered what kept my parents together. They almost never expressed any sort of caring for one another, and certainly never any love. I think they stayed together as long as they did because they both felt unlovable and because they were working under the misguided assumption that staying together was somehow "better for the kids."

I was very close to my dad; perhaps too close. He had trouble with boundaries and never seemed to understand what was and was not acceptable to share with his children. I have three sisters and they've all experienced his challenge with boundaries in their own ways, some more harmful than others. I was fortunate enough to not have been sexually abused by him, that I remember, though I can't say the same for my sister(s). I seemed to catch his good side more than his bad side, and we would talk for hours upon hours, exploring life's mysteries and daring to understand the world without limits. Though he renounced religion, he still deeply believed in the power of faith. A mustard seed of faith is enough to move mountains, he'd remind me. I believed it, too.

As I grew beyond childhood, puberty hit me hard. I was already a social outcast because I was good at school and shy, so the other kids thought I was stuck up. As the youngest of three at a time when my parents were always exhausted, I felt like a burden on others; a pest. Then, I started growing unsightly thick and dark body hair by the age of 10, and I hit such a huge growth spurt that I went from one of the shortest kids to being taller than my teacher in the space of a couple years. And as if that wasn't enough, I was also gifted with a nose that took me forever to grow into and an obscene amount of acne. My body became my worst enemy.

It didn't help that my dad would make fun of me for things like not shaving or going bra free. My appearance was always commented on, even while just at home. Other kids would call me pizza face, and even thought it was funny to run from me at recess, proclaiming that I was a giant. I was ugly and no one could let me forget it.

After years of this, I decided it had to stop. Going into high school, I wore tight-fitting, uber feminine clothes, did my hair and makeup like a pro and pushed myself to be outgoing. I shuffled around from one boyfriend to the next, too scared of losing love and attention to speak up when I felt violated. I had felt so unlovable for so long that, like my parents, I lost my self-love and I would do anything for "love." I would be whoever I thought they wanted me to be, and I would never complain or raise concerns, or talk about how I felt. All of my actions were motivated by fear of losing love, and I needed love to come from someone else because I couldn't find it in myself.

When I look back on the things I went through, it's disappointing that I didn't value myself enough to stop them. Each step of the way, I could have chosen different paths. I could have gotten out of unhealthy relationships or at least worked with them to make them better. I could have asked for help from my parents, sisters or friends. Instead, I stayed silent, or acted like things were fine when they weren't; or worse, actively fought for things I didn't want just so I could live up to this persona I thought would be more worthy of love than myself.

I compromised so much of myself, and buried myself down so deep that I stopped feeling anything. I lost nearly all of my friends, my parents divorced, my grandparents died and I allowed, and practically encouraged, myself to be the victim of sexual abuse again and again in the space of just a few years. Suffering became like a sport, and I wanted to see how far I could go. How much I could take. I starved myself, scratched at my skin and planned my own death. I jumped down the rabbit hole and wanted to see if anyone would even try to save me. By the time anyone tried, I wished they wouldn't.

Around that time, my dad started smoking. Having grown up during the 90s when anti-smoking campaigns were inescapable, smoking a single cigarette felt akin to taking a razor blade to the wrist.

It was a suicide attempt in my mind; a cry for help. I remember sitting in his truck with him one night while he lit one up. I asked him why he would ever want to smoke. It smelled bad, gave you cancer and cost you money. I didn't see the appeal. He took a deep inhale, thought about it for a minute and said, "I know it's bad for me, and that's the point. I'm punishing myself."

That answer was something I felt I understood. I, too, had actively been punishing myself. Choosing self-harm over self-care and seeing how much bad it took to die. Curiosity kept me going. I wondered what it felt like to die and I didn't see anything keeping me alive.

I found healing in the form of art. I removed myself from "love" and instead devoted myself to creativity. Photography, drawing, theatre, music, reading and writing engulfed my day to day. I worked through my pain and found joy in it. I would still relapse into numbness and self-destruction and refuse to ask for help when I needed it, but art would help keep me alive.

Eventually I felt well enough to attempt a relationship again and managed to find someone who helped me overcome my trauma rather than contributed to it. However, despite how good he was, I still had old habits that wouldn't go away. I still feared loss of love more than I valued myself and before long, I found myself shutting down, despite my partner's unwavering love and support. The part of myself that allowed for healing, I felt I couldn't share with him. He didn't see himself as artistic and wouldn't engage with it like I did, yet he was very discriminating in his artistic tastes, to the point where I felt uncomfortable sharing that side of myself with him. I began to hide things and felt like a different and incomplete version of myself in his presence. After years of shutting myself down, and with the support of the therapist I was seeing, I ventured back out into the world of music. I joined a band, performed in local bars and wrote tons of music. I was feeling closer to myself and yet I still felt unsettled. Something was still wrong.

After Christmas in 2012, my then-husband and I were sorting ourselves out before travelling home from visiting family when I began to experience extreme stomach pains. Over the course of an evening, the pain had become unbearable. Normally the type to ignore pain and refuse medication, I had tried Tylenol, Pepto-Bismol and just about anything I could get my hands on to relieve the pain, and nothing was working. I spent that night tied to the toilet until I called my mom the next morning, shaking and weak. She told me to get myself to the hospital, which she never told me to do. She was a nurse and her medical advice was always good enough, so hearing her tell me to get to the hospital as soon as possible really shook me. It was an ordeal and a half. After being rushed between three different hospitals by ambulance and having gone through just about every possible diagnostic test, the doctors still didn't know what was wrong and they were losing me. They told me my best chance of survival was to undergo exploratory surgery, so I did.

They discovered that I had had something called a Meckel's diverticulum which had knotted up my intestines. In the process, my intestines weren't sewn up properly and I nearly died again in the recovery room. After the second surgery, I began my physical recovery. I was unable to work, unable to walk without help, unable to do anything on my own. Daily life was overwhelmingly hard and I really had to find some reason to keep living. I realized that my reason to live became the desire to live my dreams, which would start with leaving my husband.

I needed freedom to explore myself and my abilities without the fear of losing love. I had to reject external love and see what was left. I had to learn to love myself.

I moved out on my own for the first time ever, and began to explore how I wanted to live my life. I started sharing my poetry at open mics and then competing at poetry slams. I quit my job at the café at which I'd been working, and became a youth support worker at the local shelter. I started calling my mom more and reconnecting with my sisters. I explored intoxication and experimented with psychadelics. I began questioning my ideas on love, sex and relationships. I spent more time with friends and met more and more new people. Those new people taught me more about life and myself in the space of a year than I had learned in my previous 25 years on this earth. I learned how to say no, how to say yes, and how to ask for what I need. I learned how to communicate boundaries and how to pay attention to the boundaries of others. I learned how to joke and be silly, how to listen without judging or advising, and how to advise without expectation or self-interested manipulation.

Rejection is still a challenge, both to give and receive, but I am learning that it isn't always a bad thing. Sometimes it's very necessary and sometimes it doesn't actually have anything to do with me, which is relieving. Not everything amounts to me being unlovable.

I still find myself spiraling downwards from time to time, and I am learning to see those times as signs that I've been compromising myself too much. Rather than seeing struggles and challenges as proof of my unworthiness of life and love, I am seeing them as opportunities for growth. When I feel a sense of loss, I try to explore what it is I think I'm losing, and whether it is grounded in reality or fear. Not all thoughts are valuable or worthwhile to hold on to, nor are they all indicative of truth and reality. These lessons seem obvious and simple, but sometimes the obvious and simple things are the hardest to learn because they are the hardest to dissect. You either get them or you don't.

Though I have not mastered these new skills, I'm beginning to recognize what they look like, and though I make many mistakes, I keep on trying. I am continuously reflecting to see how I can improve. To this day, I have yet to find a fulfilling relationship that isn't held together by fear, but I'm trying not to give up. I'm trying to find that part within myself that holds unconditional self-love and nurtures it. See what it feels like and learn how to access it when I think it's gone so that even if I never find that relationship, or those relationships, of my dreams, I won't need it/them. They'll just be the icing on the cake.

* * *

*Evelyn is a storyteller through music and spoken word poetry. She uses her art to connect with others with similar stories of hurt and healing. Only through sharing stories can we truly heal ourselves.*

# Prisoner of Hope
## by Doris Turner

*Prisoners of Hope*—*that is, who in spite of afflictions (Job 13:15; Ps 42:5, 11) maintain hope in the covenant-keeping God; in contrast to unbelievers, who say,"there is no hope". Return to the stronghold, O prisoners who have the hope; this very day I am declaring that I will restore double to you.* (Zechariah 9:12).

* * *

It happened so fast, but for one split second I believed, no I *knew*, that I was looking into His eyes.

There was far more going on here than just two people staring at each other, separated by a plate glass window, with him on the street and a buffet table full of food in front of me. I will never forget it, that tender insightful moment between us.

I felt a warming sensation throughout my body, which was unaccounted for. It confirmed to me, yet again, that there is a Higher Source, a pure, profound and powerful entity watching over us. Just as this homeless man was now watching me. Watching to see what I would do, he incredibly and seemingly appeared to be observing my soul more than my physical actions.

I knew he was waiting for me to make a decision.
*I was waiting for me* to make a decision.

I had been here before, many times, observing or talking to people who live on the street. But always not being able to fully accept it. How in this day and age, 2015, was it still possible? I mean, it is no longer medieval times. It's supposed to be, appears to be, modern day society at a higher level of consciousness. And yes, I know why they were living on the street; at least I knew most of the reasons, from talking to them and working with charities who helped them over the years. But I just could never quite grasp the "how could this happen" reason.

This deep inner desire, no, it was more of a committal to help people, animals, the environment, had always been a clear and present force since I was a young girl. Unexplainable, at best, but it had always been there.

But little did I know that this very compelling desire to help others compromised my very self. Because it took me decades to realize and comprehend that - *I had to first help myself.*

Sigmund Freud's acclaimed theory of the critical influence of "nature/nurture" on a child's development tends to provide a compelling argument for most of us.

When you are raised with one parent giving you unconditional love and the other imparting only conditional love, it gets very confusing to a young child. Even as a teen, you are still confused, which then pursues you into your adulthood and the disorientation remains. On the one hand, with one parent, you feel safe and secure, your trust is high and you know that you can "be yourself" around this person; it just feels "right." On the other hand, however, you have quite the opposite scenario going on.

This then translates into mass confusion regarding LOVE – and one's take on it. You find yourself flip-flopping back and forth on everything – a continual inner struggle to comprehend, an outer appearance of being okay when not. After all, isn't love – well – love? Does it not reap the same results when given or received?

In later years, I happened to come across this passage about childhood that fully resonated with me. It stated *"if a child is not taught self-esteem, self-worth and self-respect by their parent(s), then it is most difficult for them to know what it is or even ever acquire it. They usually don't."* That was me in a nutshell. This really struck home with me. While, on the outside, I appeared to be very confident, I was quite the opposite in actuality. This got me into trouble all along the way – not with everything in my life as you would imagine that might be the case, but with my personal relationships with men.

Added to this was my extreme adoration for, and attachment to, my wonderful biological father. He was after all, in my mind, the "prototype male". The first man that I knew so well and was most familiar with. And with whom I felt *safe* in every regard. I completely and naively believed that ALL men were like him.

So coming "out of the gate" I was already "handicapped" but, for some reason, I did not let it deter me from challenging myself, learning new things, bettering myself. My willpower and inner drive kicked in despite these handicaps – for most of the time anyway.

I also wish to acknowledge that many other people have far worse handicaps from their childhood than I had, and as well, far more dire circumstances to deal with thereafter, but since this is my story, I have to convey to you what my hindrances were and how I tried to overcome them. Some of you may have had a similar situation to mine, so I imagine you can possibly relate. As well, this is not my entire story, but a portion of it.

In every facet of my life, it seemed more natural for me to give unconditional love – even to partners in my personal relationships. In no other part of my life was it ever an issue.    In giving love, I usually got it back and was not confused by the results. But by the    time I was forty and having experienced "other men" I needed more answers. So I asked a friend of mine, who happened to be a psychologist, "What was with *me*? What was *I* doing wrong?" After stating that she had worked with thousands of clients over her years in practice, and that she could "read" people, she advised me that I was too trusting, too generous, and too forgiving. While these attributes do not appear to be negatives, more truly like positives, they did continuously and negatively affect me, and my life decisions.

Over the years, when discussing our life experiences with my closest friends, I have jokingly expressed to them that I envisage that, before we come down to planet earth, God/Source gives us a choice of "Plans" to choose from. For all I know it may be true.

It goes something like this ...

**Plan A** = a successful, prosperous, wealthy, easy life with very few, if any, problems; creativity may be low to non-existent

**Plan B** = a less successful, less prosperous life with some problems, some creativity

**Plan C** = the worst Plan of all – most things are difficult, but a good amount of creativity

I recently came across a surprising statistic with far-reaching implications for all of us.

98% of 3 year olds who are tested for their ability to brainstorm ideas score as "creative geniuses" on the scale. But by the age of 25, that number drops to 2%. What this means is that for most of us, our **"creativity quotient"** steadily declines as we grow older.

So I bravely (more like stupidly) blurted out to God/Source that I wanted to prove to Him that I could surpass any obstacle thrown at me, that I would focus on creating – and so I would take **Plan Z** (which I came up with). And because we have freedom of will – He let me.

**Plan Z** is a very extreme Plan of all the Plans because nothing goes right, nothing ever fixes, nothing is easy, there is very little happiness, joy or money, relationships can be difficult, you always feel like you are literally living on the side of a cliff and hanging   on for dear life. It will throw many extreme struggles your way. You cannot of course experience *everything* possible, but you will be put through much more than the other Plans. But - for some reason - it allows for tons of creativity  SO – I was either a complete idiot of a soul or else truly determined to prove myself, to create, to show God/Source how much one could accomplish while enrolled in this Plan!

WOW – what was I thinking?! A total fool or else very brave! Have never been sure which it was – probably a combination of both.

I do want to be clear about the fact that while it is quite natural to blame our parents for our failings, none of this narrative is about "blame". I had to give that cause up a long time ago. Rather more about me, having to find my way and dealing with this deck of cards that I had been dealt. And oh (!) if my "Plan" theory was true, hadn't I chosen this?,

Perhaps this is why I have never (quite) given in, given up.
Perhaps because I made a promise – to Him, to myself.

Oh I have yelled and screamed and pleaded multiple times over the decades that "I cannot, WILL not take any more of this" – that "I want a new script; get me off of this stage." I now wanted Plan A to kick in! I wanted out of Plan Z faster than immediately! All just proving that He, probably, would never have created such a Plan for us.

I have likened my life's experiences to being on the mat of a boxing ring and every time I tried to get back up after being whacked down, I just kept getting whacked again. What fool keeps getting up?

Finally, I asked myself – why don't you just get out of the ring? By that, I did not mean exiting the planet, but rather taking a different approach, a better path, a more possible road. I had to think upon it – very seriously.

The new version of the Disney movie "Cinderella" has a heart-wrenching line in it, when everything was crashing down on her, and she could not see a way out of her current and dreadful life. Cinderella, who was always so hopeful and positive despite what life threw at her, was finally unable to deal with it, for she had completely lost that driving hope. While she had always been a "prisoner of hope" (as I have been), she no longer could hope. It was the night of the Prince's Ball and her step-mother and step-sisters had just left to attend it – as you know, without her. She ran into the garden, to the fountain's edge, and cried and pleaded. I remember her saying this, *"I do NOT believe anymore!"*

It was so powerful a cry for help out of utter hopelessness that I cried myself. For I had been there many, many times, and actually, was "there" yet again, at that very moment while watching this movie.

Cinderella had another great line. She was talking to the Prince as he was about to put the glass slipper onto her foot. She said *"If all that I am is enough for you, what you have always wanted, then I know    I can say I love you."*

Another powerful statement I could associate with. For it seemed, to me, that *all of me* was either never enough for a partner, or they failed to even care about recognizing all of me, my inner attributes included. The latter seemed to be the case each time. I was beyond worn out and disheartened from them admiring only my outer attributes. When did the inner qualities count for something? What about a person's substance ?

I have honestly fought and wrestled with this all of my life with personal relationships.

Because this is not my complete autobiography but rather a short version of it, I cannot submerge you into deep detail of all the traumas and dramas my life has so far given me experience with. Instead, I can say that I was always solidly immersed in Plan Z again and again.

I love this line in the book "Eat, Pray, Love" by Elizabeth Gilbert – *"I never expected life to be easy, I just didn't expect it to be so hard."*

I would completely agree with this plea after having experienced some of the most potentially debilitating circumstances that life could throw at me.

After fourteen years in a marriage that should never have taken place (which I perceived well before my wedding day), I announced to my husband that it had to end, that we both deserved our space, our happiness elsewhere, and the sharing of our children.

This did not sit well with him despite the fact that I was right and he knew it. Despite the fact that he had been cheating on me since our engagement and throughout the marriage, even when I was pregnant with his first beautiful son.

If you've ever seen the movie "Sleeping With The Enemy" – that's him. I was either not going to leave him, or I was going to pay dearly for it if I did. My Achilles tendon was/is my sons. He knew it. He attacked it and me with a vengeance that was crafted in Hell.

Because he wouldn't leave our home, I had to, and I took my sons and the dog with me. That was all I took.

My descent into Hell was about to begin.

Our custody battle was *that fierce* of a conflict and without a word of a lie, made the movie "Kramer vs Kramer" look like a Disney cartoon. And yet it was the highest-grossing film of 1979! I don't personally believe in Hell, but if it were to exist, I knew what its wrath was all about, as I had experienced it in full force during that seven-year period in my life.

It seemed I was destined to lose my two precious sons in not one, but two, custody battles. By itself, alone, this situation could cripple you – if you let it. We went through three senior court judges and a revered local psychiatrist – all of whom defiantly proclaimed under no uncertain terms, that I should have "sole custody".

I was also advised, more actually warned, by the psychiatrist, that we were dealing with a "certifiable narcissist" – my husband. The fourth and final judge's decision from the first battle actually set (I was told) a precedent in our Ontario Law books due to an absolute and completely new ruling he had made on joint custody, because of our case. I was also told by my lawyer, just before the second battle, that this same judge had been going through a custody case of his own while presiding over our original case. So he was not of a mind to give in to a mother, any mother – *his son's or me.*

The final tally on the costs was $150,000 – which is yet another story.

I had been a stay-at-home mom for about half of our marriage, having left my career to have children. How was I ever going to get through this debt? And yet, it was the least of my worries, as the threat of losing my sons required the most crucial focus and all of the strength and hope that I could muster.

When my oldest son turned eleven, he pressed for me to try for sole custody again. He faced this same judge a second time by a fluke of fate, alone with his younger brother. He literally besieged the judge to give me sole custody – finally – with no visitation ever for their father – because they *never* wanted to see him again. I walked out of that courthouse, that day, with both of my precious sons in hand – forever and irrevocably.

Add to this, in the next years, three serious long-term relationships that should also never have happened. When I was leaving one of them, and stopped to ask my partner how he could ever have let this happen, he replied to me, "Well it's like this, I had the Ferrari and now I'm getting a Lamborghini." He was of course, referring to me and the "new me" he was replacing me with.

Then, there it was, inevitably – the death of my beloved Father. That was not a great time in my life either for many reasons.

I did his eulogy. I had to; it was my last gift to him. During my reading of it, I said many things, but the most absolute was that "my Father was the only person I could ever trust with my soul." Until my sons came along – then they joined this rank.

Throughout the ensuing decades arrived a host of other tsunami waves.

Because of all of this, due to all of this, multiple times during my life, I have literally "hit the wall." Meaning, as it does, that I could not bear another minute, nor second of my life. I had my "Cinderella moment" in the garden.

For the conditions that kept pummeling at me every time I tried to creep up over the wall of life would hurl me back down it again and again.

So what am I saying in all of this?

I'm saying that you take a confused child who has been an inhabitant within both unconditional and conditional love conditions, add no or little self-esteem or self-respect, and add a great example of what men should be like, but don't allow her to ever experience that example again – plus throw into the mix Plan Z - and you've got a recipe for DISASTER!

**Yet ...**

In all of this potential for failure and/or tragedy, there was always that element of "hope" winking at me – always.

I keep hearing this line in my head that I heard someone once so profoundly say.

It tends to keep a "check" on me whenever I get feeling trapped or exhausted, or am not able to believe anymore. What if, when we finally arrive into the next life, that subsequent transitioning of our soul, we must answer this and only this question – *"So what did you do with the TIME I gave you?"*

Doesn't that *so completely* put everything into perspective?

Think about what you would say, what you could not say, what you should really have been able to say?

Would you feel you wasted this time, that you did not respect this time, that you had not considered it to be the gift, the opportunity, that it was meant to be?

Wouldn't you be so humbled by this question that any answer you gave would seem trivial, or like a complaint, an excuse or whining?

That discovery, of how you would feel at that very moment, might, should, get you up and hustling with an entirely new outlook on being alive!

I do know for certain that I have spent *far too much precious time* trying to figure out my relationships, worrying and fretting about what my partners were doing while with them (because they were always involved in destructive and selfish activities of some sort), recuperating from all the losses, financial and otherwise, and rebuilding my life after I had left them. And the very worst of times were spent licking my wounds, replaying all of the trauma over and over in my head and my heart, reiterating all of the history – my history – my nature and my nurture.

All of this wasted "time" could have been spent on far more productive and positive aspects of my life.

The very presence in my life of my tremendous sons, whom I have always been in love with and ultimately committed to, and our ongoing commitment to each other, have kept me hopeful and moving forward. They will often remind me of my own words of wisdom, imparted to them while they were growing up – "Follow your passion, figure out what you want to be, try everything possible and remember that the only failure in life is when we fail to try."

My work has also kept me achieving, and has allowed me to enhance myself. My friends, who I love and who are more like my sisters and brothers, have contributed immeasurably. And last but not least, my ever-present desire to keep creating, to keep challenging myself, to keep making conditions better somehow.

Have I been in the same fix as Cinderella in the garden, in a storm of emotion, crying out that "I don't believe anymore?" A resounding YES! But I know for certain that I truly NEVER did *quite* give up HOPE! I NEVER gave up believing in some part of me that could conquer the worst scenarios that life threw at me!

I can attest to you all that – there is HOPE even in Hell.

Somehow, despite all of this, and flashing forward to the current day, I've managed to create and sustain my own consulting business (for 26 years) and get through two horrendous custody battles. I've managed to get into, and out of, several personal disempowering relationships, nurture two wonderful sons on my own, support them through university and their multiple world travel opportunities, get involved in various charities and sports activities over the years, and more recently, have been blessed to see my oldest son get married and my youngest get engaged.

So, I wonder what all I might have accomplished if I'd only had self-esteem, and was much less confused, both during my personal relationships and in other life situations.

But I've witnessed for real that if I had not hung on, if I had not kept going, I would not have lived to see the "miracle(s)" that occurred thereafter – however long it took.

So back to the proclamation I declared at the beginning of this story, *"I had to first help myself."*

I would now add to that *"I secondly or simultaneously had to also forgive myself and focus upon myself as readily as I did others."*

I am for certain, a continuing, practicing – **Prisoner of HOPE.**

My earnest wish for you is that you will be too.

And despite the plate glass window separating me from that man on the street, it could not (nor could the rules of the restaurant) keep me from filling a linen dinner napkin with food from the buffet and taking it out to him. We locked eyes again for a second time. He didn't have to say a word, I didn't expect anything, but he did speak to me. In that fleeting single moment I knew I had given him *the smallest seed of hope.*

If you believe you may also have enrolled into "Plan Z", I hope you can continue with the same gusto with which you signed up for it!

**And above all else** – remember this – and think conscientiously upon your answer …….

**What are you doing with the *TIME* He gave you?**

**What will you tell Him when He asks?**

* * *

*Doris has been operating a successful Consulting Firm for the past 26 years and has nurtured two astonishing and courageous sons on her own. They have also greatly contributed to nurturing her.*

*She has always "known" she was supposed to write.*

*But it took 3 decades to finally let this moment happen, just proving that it's never too late to do what you want to do, to do what you know you should do. It also took someone reminding her that "she had a lot to say since she was 7" and she knew it.*

*Being involved in and/or reading multitudinous sources of spiritual growth writings for decades, plus riding out her own life experiences, has enabled Doris to "allow / forge"  a paradigm shift within her, so that she can share her discoveries and hope with others.*

*She has worked with various charities over the years and is focused these days on environmental groups and their missions.*

*She is also going to continue  ~ ~ ~  writing.*

*Doris currently resides in Waterloo, Ontario and visits her sons in Europe at every moment she can.*

Are you interested in writing for an upcoming volume of *Sharing*?

Volume 4, an anthology of men's empowerment stories, will be published in November 2016.

Volume 5, an anthology of women's empowerment stories, will be published in November 2017.

For more information, contact lisa@onethousandtrees.com or visit www.sharinganthologies.com.